Pra

HEALING

Prayer-Centered
HEALING

Finding the God Who Heals

RICK MATHIS, PH.D.

Liguori
LIGUORI, MISSOURI

Published by Liguori Publications
Liguori, Missouri
http://www.liguori.org

Library of Congress Cataloging-in-Publication Data

Mathis, Richard S.
        Prayer-centered healing : finding the God who heals / Rick
Mathis.
                p.   cm.
        ISBN 0-7648-0660-2 (pbk)
        1. Spiritual healing. 2. Prayer. I. Title.

BT732.5 .M385 2000
234'.131—dc21   00–029603

Printed in the United States of America
04 03 02 01 00   5 4 3 2 1
First Edition

Contents

Why Me?

SEVERAL YEARS AGO Tony was dying from lung cancer. He decided to undergo surgery for the condition, although he knew the chances that it would be successful were very, very small. He could have felt sorry for himself as he prepared for the surgery. "Why me?" he could have asked. Instead, he did something else. He prayed.

He knew that he wasn't the only one praying. His wife, Jessica, was also praying, as were several members of the church they attended. A veteran of the Korean War who had seen many of the harsh realities of life, Tony nonetheless believed in the power of prayer. He hoped that it would make a difference.

And something did happen. The surgery was successful. The prayers he and others had prayed for were answered. Still, one question weighed upon his mind. "What's next?" he thought to himself. What was he to do now that he had been healed? Was there some reason God had spared him from cancer? What could he possibly do?

This began a period of reflection for Tony in which he learned many things about himself and about life. He began to wonder what he could do for others. He started to consider things like humility and kindness, and how he might become, in terms I will use later in the book, a *healing healer*. In acting according to his thoughts he began to experience, through grace, an even deeper sense of healing.

"Why me?" This question is probably asked by anyone facing a serious illness. Sometimes the answer is easy to find. Illness can be the result of smoking, drug or alcohol abuse, a poor diet, or risky personal behavior. At other times the answer is not readily available. An illness can come out of nowhere.

Whatever the answer to the question, another one arises immediately after it. What's next? Many times the answer to this question involves a complicated array of medical choices. There is also mounting evidence to suggest that there is another dimension to this question. Many books and articles attest to the effectiveness of prayer when used in addition to medical treatments. These are being written not by faith healers, but by medical professionals. "What's next?" can be answered not only by considering medical options, but by turning to prayer and faith as well.

As we see with Tony's experience, "What's next?" is a question not only for the sick, but for the healthy and the healed as well. Answering the question in this context is a life enhancing experience. As we will see, a prayer-centered approach to life contributes to an overall improvement in the quality of life. This is true both physically and emotionally. It is also a life-changing experience. Placing Christ at the center of your life heals something far more important than your physical body. It heals your soul.

This book answers the question of "What's next?" for both the sick and the healthy. If you are ill, there are certain practices that might help you. You will see that prayer, for example, has been linked to improved health outcomes. If you are well, then you will find practices that could help you stay that way. All of this, of course, is not meant to replace medical treatment in any way, shape, or form. If you are sick, seek medical help. What I do advocate are spiritually based practices that seem to correlate with health and well-being and can augment modern medicine.

"Why me?" and "What's next?" are also two questions I asked myself as I worked on this book. Why have I spent more than a year researching, thinking, and talking to people about prayer, faith, and healing? I do not suffer from any serious illness. The medical complaints that I do have are minor. Why should I write a book on faith and healing?

In answering this I am reminded of a story about a man who felt called to become a minister. The church in which he wanted to be ordained had a fairly elaborate interview and selection process for potential clergy. He was not sure how he was going to answer all of the questions that would be involved. When the time finally arrived and he was asked why he wanted to go into ministry, the man simply said, "Because that's what God wants me to do."

This is also the best answer for why I undertook the task of writing this book. As I contemplated reasons for my desire to write about prayer and healing, I kept coming back to that reason. It is true that I did have some background for the topic. I have long been interested in studies showing the effectiveness of prayer in healing. I had read, for example, Larry Dossey's *Healing Words: The Power of Prayer and the Practice of Medicine* and Bernie Siegal's *Love, Medicine, and Miracles*. I was also working in an area that assesses the merits of new medical technologies. This helped me to understand and appreciate the various studies on prayer, faith, and healing. Finally, I had just spent several months researching and writing *The Christ-Centered Heart*.[1] This taught me a great deal about how Jesus can heal afflictions associated with our stressful and much-too-busy age.

With the question of "Why me?" behind be, "What's next?" immediately arose. How could I best add to an area as diverse and increasingly well studied as prayer and healing? I noticed something unusual as I waded through the ocean of material on the topic. I saw that there was quite a bit written on the benefits of faith and prayer from a medical standpoint. I also noticed that there was quite a lot written concerning ways to pray and methods to heal. What I didn't see were enough bridges being built between these two areas. One goal of mine became that of taking the best from these two areas and recommending devotional practices consistent with what I found in the scientific literature. This would be helpful to people searching for ways to put the results of the research into practice.

Another goal of mine became equally important. Originally I had wanted to write more of a research-based book. Something seemed missing from that, however. "You need to be a witness to healing, and not just a reporter of it," as one friend of mine said. That sentiment haunted me throughout the year I worked on this book. An old-fashioned, introverted researcher by nature, it would have been easy for me simply to stay with books and articles on the topic. Instead, I sought out those who had been healed by prayer, as well as attended healing services.

Did I become a witness? I did. I became a witness in the deeper sense captured by contemporary Christian usage. I felt and saw the work of the Holy Spirit. It was present when I talked to those who had been healed, just as it was there when I witnessed people being prayed for with hands laid upon them.

"What's next?" became a year of reading literature on prayer and healing, talking to those who had experienced healing, and attending healing services. It concluded by my taking steps to incorporate what I had read and heard about into my personal life. I began to pray for ailments and for attitudes that I wanted to be rid of. I also prayed for others more earnestly than I had in the past. While still new at this, I do see results. More importantly, I feel a greater sense of the presence of the Holy Spirit in my life.

I write this book in hopes that you, too, will experience the Holy Spirit in your daily life. The book has that specific goal in mind. It is structured so that you may use it as a guide towards putting into practice healing devotions. Chapter 1 looks at the fact that we are all broken and ailing in some way. This leads to a number of questions, such as why good people suffer and what could be the purpose of illness. I attempt to answer such questions from a scriptural standpoint. Chapter 2 continues the use of the Scriptures by examining Jesus' healing miracles in the gospels. This is so a biblical basis for healing may be established. Chapter 3 discusses the growing amount of medical literature concerning prayer, faith, and healing, while Chapter 4 looks specifically at conclusions that can be drawn from works on AIDS and cancer. Chapter 4 also compares biblical views on suffering with those of Buddhism in order to better highlight a Christian approach to this topic. Chapter 5 looks specifically at prayer and healing and offers an approach called "the prayer of faith" as found in the works of Agnes Sanford. The idea of becoming a healer of others, and the health consequences of that, is explored in Chapter 6. Chapter 7 mentions further elements of putting into practice healing devotionals. This chapter encourages readers to look at ideas such as giving and receiving in a new light. It also draws from traditional religious practices to offer ideas on how to establish personal devotions of healing. This is continued in Chapter 8. This chapter offers simple ways of living within the healing presence of God.

At the conclusion of each chapter are thoughts on how to apply the chapter's contents to your life. This, I hope, will be a healing journey for you in which you feel a growing sense of God's presence in your life. We will go step by step together, working first from our human condition, next to the Scriptures, and then to conclusions and ideas based upon modern studies. The book is meant to be a guide; that is, a pointer to the deeper and richer personal healing experience you can have with God.

There are a few other things I would like to say before we get started. These concern the troubling issue that faces any writer on prayer, faith, and healing. Why is it that devout people are not always healed through prayer and faith? I discuss this question at various points throughout in the book. Discussing it in the beginning, though, helps you to see my particular approach to the subject of prayer, faith, and healing.

Like anything else, we can easily make mistakes by focusing on one aspect of faith. A lot of errors take place in thinking that faith in God will always lead to perfect health. All good people, and even the saints, get sick and die. In this book we will see that there are consistencies between faith and health, and that there are times that when people pray, they are healed.

Such things, I believe, are pointers to a deeper truth. The deeper truth is that Jesus is our ultimate healer. By that I mean that in redeeming us Jesus heals us as well. We find this "healing of the soul" now, but will have a deeper experience of it in heaven. We should not mistake these pointers, these earthly miracles, for the ultimate miracle that awaits us. Remember, too, that Jesus' mission was not solely that of performing physical healing.

"Jesus healed people on his way to something else," as one healing advocate, King Oehmig, told me. That statement speaks volumes in terms of understanding the place of healing in Jesus' ministry. Physical healing was one thing Jesus did, but not the only thing.

Open yourself, then, as you read this book, both to the possibility of physical healing and to the certainty of deeper healing that awaits us in Christ.

There are many people to thank in writing this book. Not the least among these is my wife, Karen, and my children, Lee and Erica. They are a constant source of healing love and support. I would also like to thank Richard Mullis, William Bishop, Frank Adkins, and Jim Wallace for their support and friendship. My friend since graduate school days, Joe Jucewicz, has offered much wise advice on a number of topics, as has my friend and pastor, Father Carter Paden III. I learned a great deal from conversations with Father King Oehmig, Dr. Bill Dudley, and Bill Jenkins. John Cleary at Liguori made many useful suggestions concerning both the approach and the content. I also benefited from discussions with a number of people regarding their own healing experiences or those whom they know. I used many of these in the book, though I often changed names and identifying circumstances in order to protect their anonymity.

One final note. There were two glaring tragedies that took place in our national culture as I wrote this book. There were others, of course, but these stand out. One was the killing of several students at Columbine High School in Colorado. Another was the killing of several people by a disgruntled "day-trader" in Atlanta. As you read this book, please make it a practice to pray for the victims of such tragedies, and to look for ways to help and to heal those around you. Perhaps in doing so you will find yourself called to be a healer. We need them.

Are You Broken?

ANYONE WHO HAS BEEN INVOLVED in medicine knows of the countless number of things that can go wrong with a person. This contributes to the sometimes humorous tendency of those beginning the study of medicine to see illness everywhere. Yet we do know that things go wrong. We see this in our daily lives, in observing our own health and that of others, as well as in the cold facts of statistical information. In a health-conscious society, such data is easily obtainable and provides a testimony to our mortality. We read that heart disease, the leading cause of death in the United States, claims well over 700,000 lives a year, and that there are almost 20 percent of Americans who suffer from high cholesterol. Cancer, the second leading cause of death, is responsible for more than half a million deaths a year, representing 129 deaths per every 100,000 people.

Other statistics are equally sobering. There are, for example, 20,000 deaths related to alcohol. This number doesn't even include alcohol-related traffic fatalities. And

of the 52 percent of Americans who drink alcohol on a
monthly basis, 16 percent are binge drinkers. That is,
they have five or more drinks on the same occasion at
least once a month.[1]

There are, of course, the less immediately life-threatening conditions that can and do lead to more serious
illnesses. The leading diagnosis in physician office visits,
for example, is hypertension, followed by upper respiratory infection, and bronchitis.[2] The leading disability claim
is carpal tunnel syndrome, followed by Epstein-Barr virus (chronic fatigue syndrome), and back/disk pain.[3]

Behind all such facts and figures is the truth that we
are all going to be sick, injured, or otherwise ill during
the course of our lives. Some of us, of course, will be
sicker than others. Some of our illnesses will require trips
to the doctor, while others will result in hospitalization.
If you really want to be morose about it, we also know
that we will die.

It is tempting to stop here, but there is another type of
illness that should also be mentioned. Psychological and
emotional disorders affect large segments of the popula-
tion. Depression, for example, is a growing concern from
several perspectives. The National Institute of Mental
Health's Depression /Awareness, Recognition, and Treatment (D/ART) program indicates that 17.6 million Americans suffer from depression in any given year, and that
the economic cost of depression is between $30 and $44
million each year. D/ART estimates that almost two hundred million workdays are lost to depression.[4] Importantly, there is a growing recognition that depression is a

disease hardly indicating a lack of character or a weakness of will. Such historical luminaries as Abraham Lincoln, Winston Churchill, and Meriwether Lewis are counted among depression sufferers.

The above information on physical and psychological conditions is interesting from an analytical viewpoint. Still, you may not feel that such information speaks directly to you. Pause for a moment to consider the people in your world right now. Do you know people who suffer from a debilitating physical condition? Is there anyone you know who is struggling with heart disease, or who is fighting a losing battle with cancer? Do you have friends whose lives have been destroyed either by their own substance abuse or by the substance abuse of someone close to them? Is there anyone you know who may be the victim of domestic violence? Have you ever had a friend who is so down that you do not know what to do? Chances are, you know people in several of the above categories. I know I do.

Then there is you. Are you suffering from some physical illness that interferes with your physical and emotional well-being? Is your heart troubled by a desire that can't be fulfilled or by a relationship that's not quite what you would like it to be?

All such questions bring us to the very simple question asked at the beginning of this chapter. Are you broken? Put another way, do you have physical and/or emotional difficulties that cause you problems? I don't know anything about you, but I bet you do. So do I.

If we are all broken, then it stands to reason that we

are all in need of some kind of healing. The argument of this book is that prayer is the healing salve for whatever is ailing us. This is as true for the life-threatening conditions you may be facing as it is for your more mundane, day-to-day physical and emotional difficulties. Prayer opens our hearts and souls to God's healing touch. This healing may be a tangible one in which the troubling condition simply disappears, or it may be the more spiritual healing of discernment and acceptance.

To illustrate these points, I will spend most of the rest of this chapter discussing one of the most famous instances where the healing that was sought for did not happen. I want to be very clear in stating that prayer-centered healing often does produce the physical and emotional improvement sought. You will see numerous examples of this in the book. We need to keep our eyes open, though, to the fact that healing does not always happen and that illness *may* have a particular meaning for the sufferer.

The incident we will deal with here is that of Saint Paul's thorn in his flesh. If ever there was a good and faithful Christian, it was Saint Paul. Yet his prayers did not produce the desired result of healing. He wrote about it this way:

> *Therefore, to keep me from being too elated, a thorn was given me in the flesh, a messenger of Satan to torment me, to keep me from being too elated. Three times I appealed to the Lord about this, that it would leave me, but he said to me, "My grace is sufficient for you, for power is made perfect in weakness." So,*

I will boast all the more gladly of my weaknesses, so that the power of Christ may dwell in me. Therefore I am content with weaknesses, insults, hardships, persecutions, and calamities for the sake of Christ; for whenever I am weak, then I am strong (2 Cor 12:7–10).

Behind this statement is a general theological truth. Every line of the above quote contains the fact that we should place God at the center of all things. This recognition begins a radical change in the way life is viewed. My weaknesses and afflictions are merely part of my human nature. As a human being, I am going to have imperfections, both physically *and* emotionally. If my attitude about these imperfections comes from a self-centered view, then I am going to experience a great deal of frustration. The more they are able to come from an attitude centered on God, the more bliss and less frustration I will feel. To use Saint Paul's words, "Whenever I am weak, then I am strong." In other words, when I recognize my own weakness, my own humanity, then I have the ability to find God and to live within the power of God's grace and strength.

Now, before we get too deeply into philosophical and theological questions, let's pull back and find the practical application of this. In fact, the practical application is quite rich. It touches upon both the reason for our brokenness as well as the "cure." Let's look at some basic truths that derive from Saint Paul.

First, we all are going to suffer physically and emotionally. Although I have already said this, it bears repeating. Suffering is our lot as human beings. We often ignore this basic fact as we live our lives, and it's probably healthy that we do. Too long and intense a focus on suffering is not going to lead to a very healthy attitude. Still, we need to come back to this point occasionally so that false notions about the nature of our lives do not mislead us.

This point is especially true from a spiritual perspective. It is important to remember that no matter how often we pray, the kind of prayers we pray, or how prayerfully we live our lives, we are going to suffer. Saint Paul and his thorn are living examples of this.

Second, we are going to die. Permit me to take yet another step down this dark path. In addition to physical and emotional pain, we are going to suffer physical death. This is our lot as mortals. Perhaps it might even be viewed as our greatest weakness. It is sometimes fruitful to look at life from the perspective of our ultimate physical death. It helps us to bring problems and troubles into sharper view, and to think about what we want our experience of life to be like.

One important aspect of our eventual death is its implications for thinking about healing. No matter what happens to us, no matter how many miraculous healings we may experience in our lives, we are going to die. Ultimately, our bodies will not be physically healed. Think about Lazarus, whom Jesus raised from the dead. As mi-

raculous as that was, we don't have any indication that
Lazarus went on to live forever. Lazarus eventually died
a final, physical death.

So if one takes the erroneous view that a failure to be
healed is God letting us down, then we are all going to be
let down. At some point our time is up. If we want to
view healing accurately, we've got to stop looking at ourselves as the center of all things. That just isn't the way
things are. Saint Paul is well aware of this, for it is all
part of being a "weak" human.

Third, a sinister element exists. As if the above were not
bad enough, Saint Paul mentions something else to be
wary of in our struggles as human beings. It is something that we are not entirely comfortable discussing in
our modern age. Saint Paul says that his thorn is a "mes-
senger" from Satan. By that I think he means that the
thorn is an event that could easily turn him to become
negative, angry, and bitter. The failure of the thorn to be
removed might easily lead him to reject God.

This raises a larger question for us. Does Satan exist
and does this dark force act in the world? We know that
Saint Paul thinks so. In his letter to the Ephesians he encourages his readers to put on the full armor of God.
"For our struggle is not against enemies of blood and
flesh," Paul writes, "but against the rulers, against the
authorities, against the cosmic powers of this present darkness, against the spiritual forces of evil in the heavenly
places" (Eph 6:12).

Speaking only from personal experience, I do think

that there is an evil force that can influence us. Its influence is often subtle, but nonetheless destructive. Today psychologists might see a person's rage as the result of getting caught up in such emotions as hatred and anger. Still, from living with myself and observing others, it seems as if the slide into rage is often too easy. Perhaps it is illustrative that in the Bible we often run up against Satan in the form of demonic possession, or as a tempter. We are all the more easily tempted or "possessed" when we are strongly emotional about something.

All of this is to say that I believe a dark force exists and plays upon our weaknesses. Saint Paul acknowledges this.

Fourth, we are broken. Let's review what we've talked about thus far. We suffer, we die, and we are subject to the influences of an evil force. This is not a particularly pleasing picture. With this going on, how can we not be broken?

This perspective is well captured in a sermon by Cistercian monk Matthew Kelty. Speaking in the Abbey of Gethsemani, Kelty talks about a stray dog that had wandered into the monastery. She was dirty, hungry, and badly wounded with a broken rear leg and a chewed up ear. Worse than this, the dog's frightened demeanor suggested that she had been beaten frequently, and hard. Her fear was so great that no one could get near without her cowering in terror.

With a little love and feeding, the dog got better and was able to love life again. Kelty saw revealed in the dog

something about human nature. Towards the end of his
homily on the experience with the stray, Kelty asks:

> *For is not each one of us in some way just like that*
> *wandering dog? Have we not been bruised and beaten*
> *by life? Been chewed up? Knocked around? Do we*
> *not all limp one way or other? Is there any one here*
> *bold enough, foolish enough to maintain that he or*
> *she is sound? Whole and perfect? Has not the evil*
> *one rather left his mark on us all?*[5]

We are, I think, like stray dogs when we think about
it. We are all suffering from broken hearts and lost dreams.
We've lost loved ones, we've not been cured in spite of
our prayers, and we've had to suffer at the hands of evil.
Like the dog that came to the monastery, we are broken.

Fifth, there is a way out of our brokenness. What do we
do about our broken situation? So far we have lamented
our nature as human beings. Doesn't that mean that we
have to resign ourselves to this nature? Doesn't a truth-
ful recognition of this lead to pessimism?

Not necessarily.

There is the possibility of a changed perspective. This
is exactly what Saint Paul is pointing towards. He says
that he "boasts" in his weakness, and that the recognition of his weakness makes him strong. What does this
mean? This is a very important question since it applies
not just to Saint Paul, but to you and me as well. What
Saint Paul is getting at here is that in recognizing my own

weakness I can yield to a higher power. That higher power is Christ. Recognition of oneself as mortal is a necessary step in the recognition of the centrality of Christ in our lives. There is someone to lean upon, to embrace, even in our weakness.

Sixth, there is grace and healing. Once we recognize our weakness, and Christ's strength, we begin to experience the grace of God in all things. There are two elements of this. First, we experience the grace of God in our relations with ourselves. As we move through the various difficulties of life, we see our weaknesses and offer them up to God. Second, we experience grace in our relationship with the world. As we move through the world, we are all going to experience unforeseen triumphs and tragedies. Healing allows us to get beyond these.

There are a couple of things that need to be said about both of these aspects of grace. As far as our own weaknesses are concerned, I think that this involves a certain kind of spiritual maturity that comes with age. It is only by spending some time with yourself that you begin to take a detached perspective. Detachment allows you to understand that you are not perfect, that there are some ways you have of dealing with the world that lead to problems, and that you may have to deal with these all of your life. For example, when I was younger I had a hard time saying that I had character flaws. I thought I was great just the way I was, and that admitting any flaws was a sign of weakness. As I aged, however, I began to see where people had difficulties with me, where I may

be hard to understand or tolerate, as well as where I have
difficulty with other people. When you see the areas where
you are not so great, where your "character" thorns are,
then you can get enough space from yourself to begin to
experience healing.

The other area of healing is that of dealing with the
externals of the world. This is a little more difficult, for
we often run up against some terrifying events. Divorce,
the death or illness of a child, the loss of a loved one, and
debilitating illnesses are examples of such events. These
are things that are difficult to deal with, and can tear
down the life of even the staunchest person. There is evidence, though, that a spiritual perspective assists in facing these difficulties. We will deal with this aspect of grace
and healing in later chapters.

Seventh, the healing sought may not happen. Our last
point is a rather difficult one. We always know what we
want to happen when we ask God for something. In healing, of course, we want the particular affliction to go
away. We have an example in the above passage of someone asking for an affliction to end and it simply not happening. Saint Paul says that he pleaded three times for
the thorn to be taken away. The thorn, however, remained. Instead, he found that God's grace is sufficient,
and that God's power is made perfect in weakness.

Paul's experience should not foster a disbelief in the
power of prayer to heal. We see instead that when a man
who enjoyed a very strong connection to God encountered an affliction, the first thing he did was to pray. And

pray. And pray again. Only after petitioning several times did he begin to see his ailment in another light. Through grace, he was able to find a purpose to his suffering.

It is impossible to come up with a rule for this type of acceptance of suffering. I do see this kind of acceptance as a form of healing. Saint Paul provides a good model for how this works. When confronted with an ailment, pray for your release from it, and keep praying if at first the prayer is not successful. There may come a time, however, when it becomes clear that the healing sought is not going to happen. At that point, search for the deeper understanding that Paul was able to attain.[6]

The seven points above combine to form the following: We are broken, and that is our nature as humans. There is, though, the very real possibility of healing. It may not be physical healing that takes place, but a deeper healing. In realizing our ultimate brokenness, we experience ultimate healing through discovering the power of the great healer.

Before concluding, let's make sure we can bring the above words and sentiments to the level of reality. Recently, I heard about the death of a woman whom my wife knew many years ago. What was uplifting, though, was something that happened during the final years of this woman's life. She had been diagnosed with cancer and had been sick for much of the last years of her life. She had a group of friends who started meeting at her house every Sunday morning during these final years. The meeting became a worship service of sorts, one that included a lot of laughter and fellowship. The meeting became the high point of the week for these people, and is now a memory they will treasure forever. Although there was not a healing from cancer, there was certainly something equally miraculous taking place. The people in this group were touched by what had happened. I dare say that there was a lot of healing even among the "brokenness" of cancer.

Though our health will fail us and our circumstances cause us stress, there is healing of all types available to us. It comes not through always focusing on what we want but by focusing upon God and living accordingly. This focus, to use another one of Matthew Kelty's sermons, leads to rapture. "Rapture," he writes, "is a quality of the pure in heart. To perceive reality in its fullness, therefore, we must be pure of heart."[7] This purity of heart can only come from the love of God. Towards the end of this sermon on purity of heart, Kelty uses words that may well describe your life from time to time, as they do mine. He talks about the joy of recognizing God no matter how we may feel. "What matter if my own heart be barren and empty, my mind a sterile waste, my own life full of fuss and fury. It does not matter. You do not need to be holy to love God. You have only to be human."[8]

You have only to be human.

Perhaps that is just another way of getting at what Saint Paul was saying. It is in loving God from our broken humanness and our need for healing that God's power is made complete. In the chapters that follow we will look at various types and manifestations of healing, many of which involve real, physical healing from such conditions as blindness, deafness, and depression. Let us not forget to love God, however, from the humanness of the afflictions that may continue.

Exercise 1: Naming the Hurt

Now that we have examined brokenness and its possible messages for us, take a moment to reflect upon your own pain. Where does it hurt? Remember that this can either be physical or emotional pain. It may also be a pain that someone you know is experiencing. After you write down the hurts that you or others are suffering from, pray silently for guidance concerning them. Write down any thoughts you may have as a result of this.

The Healing Word

I HAVE ALWAYS BEEN A SEEKER. This time my seeking brought me to the brink of despair. I was at the end of my rope. I was working for someone who took pleasure in cruelty and who was also unassailable within the organization. Working in a geographic region with a limited job market and not feeling predisposed to move, there was the added pressure of not having a readily available exit. Finally, there was my constant search for meaning in life. I was looking for just the right job, the place where I could best use whatever God-given talents I possessed.

It was really this last issue, this seeking, that caused the most stress and despair. I had placed upon myself the "requirement" that I find something, and find it soon. As I looked around my environment, however, I saw no options. I was trapped. This led to a deepening sense of depression and an irascible temperament. During this time I also contracted pneumonia, which I attributed in part to an immune system weakened by stressful days and sleepless nights.

After recovering from pneumonia, I decided to take a brief trip. On a rare, spur-of-the-moment action, I got into my car and drove to the Abbey of Gethsemani in Kentucky. This was the monastery of the late Thomas Merton, the famous monk and writer. Although the monastery was several hours away, I didn't plan the trip at all. I had no idea where I would stay or what I would eat. Worse, I had not made any arrangements to visit the monastery. I was just going to arrive.

I drove into the abbey parking lot around three o'clock in the afternoon. It was a bright late spring day with lots of sunlight still left. I walked into the modern reception area and spoke with a monk whose job it was to handle outsiders.

"I don't suppose I could take a look inside the monastery?" I asked with little confidence in my voice.

"We can't really allow that," the monk replied. "It wouldn't be a monastery then."

"I guess I could just look around the grounds on the outside," I stammered. "I'm a big Merton fan." I was trying to establish some reason for my being there, both to myself and to the monk.

"That brings a lot of 'em," he smiled. "Have you seen the statues?"

"No."

"Oh, you've got to see that. A lot of people go up there. The path is just down the road."

I left the monastery and walked down the road until I came to a small sign marking the path to the statues. As I started down the path, I berated myself for not planning this trip better. I could have called ahead to make arrangements. I knew that the abbey allowed visitors to stay for brief retreats of a day or more, provided they make arrangements beforehand. Basically, I had just driven the better part of a day only to walk down a path. After walking a good distance I noticed a small open shed, a hut of sorts, just off of the trail. I walked cautiously towards it, suspecting it to be off limits to all but the groundskeeper. I walked inside and noticed a pad of paper on a lectern. At the top of the lectern were instructions for visitors to write down whatever may be troubling them. The instructions also asked that visitors pray for their own healing and for those who had come previously. A rosary rested atop the pad.

I read the note from the most recent visitor. It was from a man whose daughter was very ill. I thought how trivial my concern was compared to his. Here was someone who had a real concern with which to deal. I took up the rosary and prayed for the man and for his daughter. Then I wrote down my own feeble request for a life of meaning. I thought about how weary I felt as I wrote. I hadn't slept well the night before, or for the last several nights for that matter. I was tired and filled with self-doubt. My all-day, spur-of-the-moment trip had only made matters worse. Still, I prayed.

I walked out of the shed and started back down the trail. Then something strange happened. I felt a lightness that I had not experienced for a long time, perhaps ever. All of my cares were suddenly lifted from me and were replaced with a deep sense of peace. I felt light in the

Spirit. This, I knew, was the result of my prayer, a prayer that I hardly expected to be answered in any way. Though I continued down the trail and gazed upon the statues, I have only a vague memory of them. It was the memory of what happened after praying in that small hut that remains with me.

This event, which happened over ten years ago, proved to be a healing one. It began a process of discovering how my concerns of the time were in large measure self-induced, the result of placing myself, and not Christ, at the center of my life. I discovered, slowly, the healing joy of practicing the presence of God.

This experience demonstrates not only the very real power of the Holy Spirit but also that prayer-centered healing is very much a part of Christianity. For why else would there be this hut on the grounds of a monastery? Why else would people stop at this hut and write down their concerns, hoping that they would find healing through prayer?

The availability of healing within Christianity has its roots in the New Testament. More importantly, it is found within the life and ministry of Jesus. What role did healing have in Christ's ministry and what does this mean to us? We will see below that healing went to the very heart of Christ's mission. As far as we are concerned, one theme you will find in this book is that we are enjoined not only to seek healing when we are ill but also, as disciples of Christ, to be healers. For me, this has been one of the most startling revelations I have had in writing this book. We will begin to see evidence of this as we look back to the healing word of the Scriptures. Let's look, then, at Jesus as a healer.

Imagine that you have a friend, a young man, who is a paraplegic. He is someone whom you love dearly, and you want nothing more than to see him healed. You hear that there is a great healer in town, someone who is performing a number of miracles. You and your friends decide to take your paraplegic friend to this healer. You form a group and take him to the building where the healer is. The crowd, however, is large, so large that you can't even make it through the door. In desperation you and your friends form a plan. You decide you'll come through the roof.

This is exactly the scene of Luke 5. We see here what must have been a very dramatic scene. A paralyzed man is slowly lowered through the roof of a building and set before Jesus. Jesus responds to the drama in kind. After debating with the Pharisees about whether he has the power to forgive sins, Jesus says to the man, "I say to you, stand up and take your bed and go to your home." Upon hearing this, the man stands up and goes home, singing praises to God all the way. The crowd witnessing this miracle says, almost in unison, "We have seen strange things today" (Lk 5:17–26).

Those were strange days. The above event says much about what was happening. Jesus had the power to heal; a power intimately tied to his role as the savior. Many people sought him out as a healer. Jesus often healed, though, not only for the sake of healing, but to demonstrate something about himself and his mission. In Luke 5 we see that the issue was also his ability to forgive sins. This claim to power was contested and eventually used against him when he was ordered to be put to death. We see the beginnings of this in Jesus' argument with the Pharisees in the scene above. We will also discover that it was healing, particularly healing on the Sabbath, which led opposing groups to initiate the series of events that eventually led to the Crucifixion.

As it is important to understand healing in the gospels, let's explore more deeply what they say about Jesus as a healer. To begin with, we know that healing was part of the predicted messiah's role, and that Jesus fulfilled this prediction. There is a very poignant moment in the gospels where John the Baptist, imprisoned by Herod and soon to be beheaded, sends two messengers to Jesus to ask if he is "the one who is to come, or are we to wait for another?" (Lk 7:20). We can read between the lines to see what was happening. John was living in what must have been squalid conditions. His very life was on the line. He wanted to know, beyond a doubt, if the appointed one had come. Jesus responds by saying, "Go and tell John what you have seen and heard: the blind receive their sight, the lame walk, the lepers are cleansed, the deaf hear, the dead are raised, the poor have good news brought to them. And blessed is anyone who takes no offense at me" (Lk 7:22–23).

It is telling that most of what Jesus said in reply to John the Baptist's question is related to healing. People, in short, were having their afflictions healed. Even more astounding, even the dead were being raised.

There was an expectation, then, that the messiah to come would be a healer. It was not simply that miracles would be performed. Jesus performed a number of miracles, from changing water into wine to walking on water. There was something unique about healing, something that went to the very heart of his mission.

Also evident in reading about Jesus' healing miracles is that the scope of his healing was very broad, as were his methods of healing. There are numerous instances of Jesus' healing power mentioned in the gospels. Time after time we read of Jesus healing the blind, the deaf, and the lame. He cured leprosy and cast demons out of those who were possessed. He even raised the dead.

Jesus' methods of healing were equally diverse. He did not simply lay his hands on each person who sought healing. There are instances where he did not do anything physically, but where someone simply reached out to touch him. This was the case with the woman suffering from excessive bleeding who touched his cloak (Mk 5:25–34). This was not the only healing by the mere touch of his cloak. The gospels also record Jesus healing in a region called Gennesaret. Mark writes that wherever Jesus went in this region, whether it be villages or cities or farms, "they laid the sick in the marketplaces, and begged him that they might touch even the fringe of his cloak; and all who touched it were healed" (Mk 6:56).

Jesus used several other methods to heal. One was simply touching the sick. Jesus, for example, merely touched the hand of Saint Peter's mother-in-law to cure her of fever (Mt 8:15). Similarly, Jesus touched the eyes of the

blind in Matthew 9:29 and 20:34. He also healed a leper
by touch in Mark 1:41. Finally, in an instance close to
touch but not quite, he touched the bier of a dead man
being carried to a funeral in Luke 7:14, and this man was
raised to life.

We also see Jesus using his saliva, or the combination
of the ground and his saliva, to heal. Mark records instances when Jesus placed his saliva on the tongue of a
man with a speech impediment and on the eyes of a blind
man (7:32–35 and 8:22–26). John 9:1–15 tells of Jesus
making a mud paste out of the ground and his saliva and
spreading it on a blind man's eyes to heal the man's blindness.

Touch, whether by someone touching Jesus or him
touching the one who would be healed, is not always
necessary to Jesus' healing. In current terminology as used
by such writers as Dr. Larry Dossey, whom we will read
about later, Jesus used nonlocal healing as well. Matthew
8:5–13 recounts a moving story of a Roman centurion
coming to Jesus and pleading with him to heal one of his
servants. At first Jesus consented to go to the man's house,
but the centurion said that he was unworthy to have Jesus
come to his home. This man's faith impressed Jesus
greatly. Jesus said, "Go, let it be done for you according
to your faith." The servant was healed, at a distance,
from that very hour. In another instance, Jesus healed a
group of lepers from a distance. He commanded a group
of ten lepers, standing some distance away, to show themselves to the priests. As they left Jesus' presence, "they
were made clean" (Lk 17:11–14).

One other means of Jesus' healing was that of a verbal command. This was used, for example, in dealing with those possessed by demons. Jesus rebuked and thereby cast out demons in such verses as Matthew 17:18 and Mark 1:23–26. Perhaps the most famous instance of this approach is Jesus' casting out of several demons, together called Legion, who were possessing a man. Jesus, at Legion's request, commanded the demons to leave the man and go into a herd of swine. Legion did so, and then the herd rushed into the nearby sea and drowned (Mk 5:1–13).

In other instances of verbal command, Jesus simply pronounced healing. This occurred in the healing of a blind man in Mark 10:51–52 when Jesus simply told the man that his faith had made him well, as well as in the case of the paralytic mentioned at the beginning of this chapter. In this last instance, Jesus simply told the man, "Stand up, take your bed and go to your home" (Mt 9:6).

We can see the ways Jesus healed and that his healing was part of his ministry. Are there other aspects of his healing that might be helpful to understand? There are two further statements that can be made about his healing miracles. The first is that faith is often part of the healing. Thus Jesus commented upon the centurion's faith when he healed his servant in Matthew 8. Mark also writes of Jesus telling a blind man whom he had healed that it was his faith that made him well (Mk 10:52). In the case of the paralyzed man who was lowered through the roof, Jesus commented on the faith of the man's friends before healing him (Lk 5:20). Finally, Jesus said to the woman who suffered from excessive bleeding and who touched his cloak, "Daughter, your faith has made you well; go in peace, and be healed of your disease" (Mk 5:34). In such instances it is as if the faith of the person in need combined in some way with the power of Jesus to produce the desired healing.

Another feature of Jesus' healing is that it often had a message. Jesus used healing to make points to those who witnessed the event. We have already seen that when Jesus healed the paralytic who was lowered through the roof, he did so by telling him that his sins are forgiven (Mk 2:5). This created a tumult amongst the scribes in the audience.

"How can you claim the power of forgiveness of sins?" the scribes surely asked.

Perceiving this, Jesus told them that his forgiveness of this man was so that they may know that the Son of Man "has authority on earth to forgive sins" (Mk 2:10).

Jesus also used healing to upbraid the Jews of the time for their lack of faith in him and to indicate that faith would create a new ministry that reached beyond them. We get an inkling that his ministry was for the sake of not only the Jews of Israel in his exchange with a woman of Syrophoenician origin. Mark 7:26–30 tells of this woman coming to ask Jesus to heal her daughter. At first Jesus was reluctant, saying that he must feed the children first (meaning the Jews) before throwing the food to the dogs (a rather graphic way of referring to all others). The woman persisted, however, insisting that even the dogs under the table eat the children's crumbs. Jesus was impressed with her persistence and reasoning, and healed her child (in another example of nonlocal healing, for the child was in bed at home). In this instance we get an indication that Jesus' ministry would reach beyond Israel.

This message is more pronounced in Jesus' healing of the centurion's servant. The centurion was obviously a Gentile, but also a man of great faith in Jesus' ministry. This faith impressed Jesus, for he said upon performing the healing that "truly I tell you, in no one in Israel have I found such faith. I tell you, many will come from east and west and will eat with Abraham and Isaac and Jacob in the kingdom of heaven, while the heirs of the kingdom will be thrown into the outer darkness, where there will be weeping and gnashing of teeth" (Mt 8:10–12). In rather ominous words, Jesus spoke of the disbelief his ministry would encounter amongst his own people.

One other aspect of Jesus' healing message has to do with healing on the Sabbath. Among the Jews of the time any work was strictly forbidden on the Sabbath. In fact, healing on the Sabbath was the very thing that caused the Pharisees and the Herodians to plot to destroy Jesus (Mt 12:14; Mk 3:6; Lk 6:11; Jn 5:16). Healing on the Sabbath allowed Jesus to show the supremacy of kindness over legalism. When a man with a withered hand approached Jesus one Sabbath, for example, Jesus asked those around him, "Is it lawful to do good or to do harm on the sabbath, to save life or to kill?" When those around him were silent, Jesus "grieved with anger" at the hardness of their hearts before healing the man's hand (Mk 3:4–5).

Jesus healed the faithful, and he often did so with a message attached to the healing. These combine to form the impression that Jesus healed to show us something. He showed us the power of faith and the supremacy of love. Jesus' healing miracles underscore the early Christian emphasis upon faith and love.

One other quality of his healing is that he often asked that the healing not be made known. In Matthew 9:27–30 Jesus orders two blind men whom he had healed not to make the healing known (although they did anyway). Similarly, Matthew 12:15–16 has Jesus curing many, but also telling them "not to make him known." Jesus heals a leper in Mark 1:40–45, but afterwards sternly orders him to say nothing to anyone. The leper, similar to the blind men, ignores Jesus' order and spread words of the healing so that "Jesus could no longer go into a town openly, but stayed out in the country; and people came from every quarter."

Before going too deeply into Jesus' possible reasons for trying to keep his healing miracles from becoming widely publicized, suffice it to say that the strategy didn't work. We see this in the following passage:

> *Jesus went throughout Galilee, teaching in their synagogues and proclaiming the good news of the kingdom and curing every disease and every sickness among the people. So his fame spread throughout all Syria, and they brought to him all the sick, those who*

were afflicted with various diseases and pains, demoniacs, epileptics, and paralytics, and he cured them. And great crowds followed him from Galilee, the Decapolis, Jerusalem, Judea, and from beyond the Jordan (Mt 4:23–25).

Why this ultimately unsuccessful concern for secrecy? One reason readily comes to mind. He may have been concerned that the crowds following him would become too large, making it difficult for him to move about and conduct his ministry. Perhaps knowing that healing would be linked to his eventual crucifixion, Jesus also had to be careful lest he become too widely known as a healer. Too much fame too soon would shorten the time of his ministry.

I think this explanation has some validity. It also points to one other concern. I think it was important not to allow the physical healing of the sick to overtake the main reason for Jesus' appearance, which was our redemption. Jesus' healing of individuals was not to eclipse his mission as the ultimate Healer of sins.

Preventing this eclipse was, I'm sure, a rather difficult thing to do. Jesus was working against the natural desire of humans to be physically well. It is difficult to stay focused on redemption when consumed with concern about physical health. Jesus could heal both our physical afflictions and our broken nature as human beings. In doing the one, however, he needed to be careful not to allow the other, stronger healing, to become lost. This is an important lesson to remember today.

Now that we have identified some of the individual features of Jesus' healing, let's step back to see if we can get a glimpse at the entire picture. We have seen that the predicted messiah was going to be a healer, and that Jesus understood his healing as fulfilling this prediction. The most compelling evidence of this is his response to John the Baptist's question of whether he was "the appointed one." As far as his healing was concerned, Jesus healed all types of illnesses, including death itself. Jesus did not use any one technique in healing. Sometimes he touched, at others he was touched. For those with sensual impairments (blind, deaf, and/or mute) he sometimes made a paste using the ground and his saliva. He once healed lepers from a short distance, and they actually became healed on their way to a priest after they had left his presence. Others were healed at a greater distance. He also healed by pronouncement or rebuke, especially when dealing with the possessed.

Although Jesus did not always comment on why he healed a particular person, there were times when he stated that a person's faith had healed them. Jesus also used healing to make a point. Healing played a role in refuting the overemphasis upon the law (healing on the Sabbath), as well as Jesus' demonstration of his power to forgive sin. Additionally, Jesus' healing of Gentiles showed that his message would reach beyond Judaism. Finally, though healing was part of Jesus' popularity among the people of the time, Jesus sought to keep it a secret in some instances. This indicates that while healing was important, it was not the central message of his ministry.

This picture helps us to construct a possible place for healing in our lives today. Although we certainly can't claim to have any status as messiah, it is worth considering why healing would be so much a part of the predicted savior's life. If Christ could heal, might it not be expected that some of the disciples who followed him, both during his time and afterward, would in some form or fashion have the gift of healing as well? If the answer to this question is yes, then it also stands to reason that the methods of healing would be similar to what we find Jesus doing. That is, by touch, being touched, command or rebuke, and by nonlocal healing. Faith on the part of the healer and the healed would also be important. Finally, healing would not be considered as the most important aspect of a Christian, but rather a mere part or aspect of the Faith. It would never be used to obscure the deeper message of the final, ultimate healing that Jesus offers to each of us. It is a part of the ministry, but not the whole part, and not even the most important part.

If the above is true, then we would expect to see this echoed in the writings of the apostles. We can, in fact, see the above themes both in the gospels and in the epistles. For example, we know that Jesus expected his disciples to heal. Matthew has Jesus telling his disciples to proclaim the good news. As they went forth, they were to "cure the sick, raise the dead, cleanse the lepers, cast out demons" (10:8). In essence, they were to perform the same healing miracles as Jesus. We also find the following passage in Matthew, which contains the "faith of a mustard seed" statement mentioned at the beginning of this chapter:

> *When they came to the crowd, a man came to him,*
> *knelt before him, and said, "Lord, have mercy on my*
> *son, for he is an epileptic and he suffers terribly; he*
> *often falls into the fire and often into the water. And*
> *I brought him to your disciples, but they could not*
> *cure him." Jesus answered, "You faithless and per-*
> *verse generation, how much longer must I be with*
> *you? How much longer must I put up with you? Bring*
> *him here to me." And Jesus rebuked the demon, and*
> *it came out of him, and the boy was cured instantly.*
> *Then the disciples came to Jesus privately and said,*
> *"Why could we not cast it out?" He said to them,*
> *"Because of your little faith. For truly I tell you, if*
> *you have faith the size of a mustard seed, you will say*
> *to this mountain, 'Move from here to there.' And it*
> *will move; and nothing will be impossible for you"*
> (Mt 17:14–20).

We may gather from this, then, that the disciples were empowered to heal. We should also note, once again, that faith was involved.

The fact that the disciples healed is found outside of the gospels as well. Healing is among the works of the disciples as recorded in the Acts of the Apostles. True to Matthew 10, the disciples cured the sick, cast out de-mons, and even raised the dead. Like Jesus, they used a variety of methods, from touch to staring intently and rebuke.[1] Faith was also important in their healing. Saint Paul, for example, heals a paralytic after seeing that he had, "the faith to be healed" (Acts 14:9).

Healing, though important, was not the most important element of the early Church. Saint Paul writes of
healing as being one among several gifts of the Spirit. In
his first letter to the Corinthians we find the following:

> *Now there are varieties of gifts, but the same Spirit;*
> *and there are varieties of services, but the same Lord;*
> *and there are varieties of activities, but it is the same*
> *God who activates all of them in everyone. To each is*
> *given the manifestation of the Spirit for the common*
> *good. To one is given through the Spirit the utterance*
> *of wisdom, and to another the utterance of knowl-*
> *edge according to the same Spirit, to another faith by*
> *the same Spirit, <u>to another gifts of healing by the one</u>*
> *<u>Spirit</u>, to another the working of miracles, to another*
> *prophecy, to another the discernment of spirits, to*
> *another various kinds of tongues, to another the in-*
> *terpretation of tongues. All these are activated by one*
> *and the same Spirit, who allots to each one individu-*
> *ally just as the Spirit chooses* (1 Cor 12:4–11, under-
> line added).

Saint Paul wrote this, no doubt, in recognition that
the Spirit gives various gifts, and that a person receiving
one type of gift should not feel superior to others or cause
dissension because of it. Paul makes this argument to lead
us up to his stunning and powerful pronouncement of
love as the greatest of gifts in 1 Corinthians 13. At the
end of chapter 12 Paul writes: "Are all apostles? Are all
prophets? Are all teachers? Do all work miracles? Do all

possess gifts of healing? Do all speak in tongues? Do all interpret? But strive for the greater gifts. And I will show you a still more excellent way" (1 Cor 12:29–31). Healing, then, is a gift of the Spirit. It is one gift among many, and certainly not as important or as excellent as love.

The ability to heal continued with the disciples, and, as we will see, continues to this day. In this regard, the actions of Jesus and the disciples speak directly to us. Healing is a consequence of a relationship with God. It can be brought about in many ways, but is certainly assisted by faith. Finally, the ability to heal is a gift that some possess to a greater degree than do others. It is also a gift, if we take Jesus' statements to his disciples seriously, that we are all enjoined to use. This gift, however, should not be enshrined as the most important aspect of Christianity. The final gift, the one that has the ability to heal deeply in spite of our physical circumstances, is God's love for us.

All of this is encapsulated in some very practical advice we find in the epistle of James. He writes:

> *Are any among you suffering? They should pray. Are any cheerful? They should sing songs of praise. Are any among you sick? They should call for the elders of the church and have them pray over them, anointing them with oil in the name of the Lord. The prayer of faith will save the sick, and the Lord will raise them up; and anyone who has committed sins will be forgiven. Therefore confess your sins to one another,*

and pray for one another, so that you may be healed.
The prayer of the righteous is powerful and effective
(Jas 5:13–16).

Healing was very much a part of the mission of the
disciples, and one of the practices of the early Church.
Although Jesus had more healing power than did the disciples, it is true that healing in his name continued after
he was gone. This has a direct application for us, for there
is nothing from the Scriptures to suggest that healing
would stop after the first generation of Christians. Healing continues as a possibility for us, a very real power,
just as the power of the Holy Spirit remains.

We have established a biblical basis for healing, one
that shows the methods, the uses, and the place of healing. From here we will take a look at the modern manifestations of healing. We will see that faith continues to
bring about physical healing. More importantly, faith
brings about the redemptive healing of our souls in our
individual encounter with Jesus. The central element in
these processes is prayer, for in prayer we petition for
healing, and in prayer we find a healing communion with
the Triune God.

Exercise 2: Being in the Presence

Read Mark 5:25–34. Imagine yourself to be in a situation similar to that of the woman who touched Jesus' cloak. Imagine yourself to be in a crowd, concerned about whatever affliction or problem you may be having. Prayerfully see yourself working your way through the crowd, wanting to be close to the great Healer. As you draw near, reach out and touch his cloak and feel the healing power go into your body. Experience Jesus turning to you and gazing lovingly upon you. Hear his kind words as he praises your faith and pronounces that your sins are forgiven. Open your heart to this love and then joyfully go on your way.

The Nice Connection

AMANDA IS A NORMAL, forty-something soccer mom living in a moderately sized city in the Southeast. She spends most of her time doing the things that people with growing children do. She gets her children up in the morning, makes them breakfast, and then waves good-bye as her husband takes them to school on his way to work. She pursues a variety of interests and activities, including work with the PTA and volunteering at the local community kitchen.

Everything is normal except one thing. Every Wednesday she follows behind her minister as he conducts a small healing service after holy Communion. The minister administers unction and she walks behind him laying her hands on the people at the rail. The people at the altar have a variety of ailments, some serious and others fairly minor. Although not everyone she touches is healed, there are times when the miraculous happens. There are times when people are cured.

Amanda approached her minister about doing such a

service after a profound healing took place in her life. She had cancer. The doctors had given her all of the chemotherapy she could withstand, but to no avail. She was in the hospital, on her deathbed, when her minister was called in to administer last rites. He did so, not expecting ever to see her alive again in this world. He received a surprise phone call from the hospital a few days later. Amanda wanted to see him.

When he walked into the room, he could tell that she was different. Ordinarily shy and reserved, she had become more assertive. She told her physician that she was through with the chemotherapy, that she neither wanted nor needed it anymore. To everyone's surprise, she left the hospital a short time later and experienced a complete recovery.

After a few months passed, she approached her minister with a startling request. She was convinced that she now had the gift of healing and wanted to find a way to use this gift. She knew that the church offered a midweek eucharistic celebration and she saw this as an opportunity for God's healing power to work through her.

Her minister, however, was skeptical, and his skepticism caused her to doubt as well. Both of them tried to ignore this feeling she had. Healing, while obviously part of the Church's tradition, is not something that is currently emphasized. Amanda reluctantly agreed to put her feelings on hold.

Then the minister himself got an odd feeling. He felt a nagging sense that maybe there was something to Amanda's request and that perhaps he had too readily discounted it. Much to his own surprise, he consented to allow her to walk behind him after the Eucharist.

To Amanda's and the minister's astonishment, some miraculous events did occur. A few people reported soon afterward that they had been healed. Others said that while they were not completely healed, their symptoms were greatly eased. After a few of these occurrences the minister decided to make Amanda a permanent part of the service. While not everyone attending these services is healed, it happens enough to convince even the most skeptical that something special is going on here.

What are we to make of this? How does this fit with the first chapter's emphasis on our broken human nature? The fact is that in spite of our mortality, there is evidence that prayer-centered healing exists. We've seen accounts of this in the Scriptures. Today this evidence is found both in anecdotal accounts as well as scientific, double-blind studies. The weight of evidence is beginning to show something rather astonishing. What many consider miraculous could in fact be fairly commonplace. Moreover, evidence is mounting to show a nice connection between faith, healing, and wellness.

Let's begin this discussion with a less formally scientific area and move on to the rigors of rigid clinical studies. I encourage you to try the following experiment. Although not the same as a formal scientific study, this experiment will probably produce interesting results. Try asking a few people if they or someone they know has ever experienced anything like an unexplained or spiritual-based healing. As you try this "experiment," also keep your eyes and ears open for anything you may come across by "chance." Listen for any conversations you may hear or newspaper accounts you may read.

When I tried this experiment I encountered all manner of things. I heard about individuals or the friends and relatives of individuals who had been prayed for and who had "beaten the odds" with respect to all kinds of life-threatening illnesses. I also heard about more subtle types of healing, such as when people received quiet assurance about a particular issue in their life. Finally, I encountered stories such as the one I wrote of in the first chapter where a group of people got together each week at the home of a terminally ill friend. Here, though physical healing had not taken place, there was a deeper healing experienced by the group.

It is my experience that such events are not as rare as you might expect. It is interesting, for example, that when someone writes a book about miracles, angels, or other such topics they tend to receive a flood of letters from people claiming to have had similar experiences. Many times these writers are able to publish sequels to their books that are nothing but letters from readers recounting their experiences. Granted, some of these people are probably just trying to get their names into print, while others may have had experiences that can be explained by more natural phenomenon. Still, the sheer number of responses that such authors receive attests to something happening.

But isn't this all merely anecdotal evidence, lacking the rigor of scientific study? Surely faith-based wellness and healing cannot stand up to scientific scrutiny. As a matter of fact, it does. There are three recent books written by physicians that discuss in detail scientific experiments conducted in this area. They are *The Faith Factor* by Dale Matthews, *Healing Words* by Larry Dossey, and *Love and Survival* by Dean Ornish. Each of these books draws from many scientific studies to indicate the measurable positive health outcomes of such things as attendance in worship services, prayer, and compassion.

Let's take a look at these three aspects of the spiritual life as they apply to healing. The impact of religious involvement upon health has received an increasing amount of study over the years. In *The Faith Factor*, Dr. Matthews references several such studies. He sites one examination of the literature that found "over 75 percent of 325 studies of different types, undertaken by hundreds of different researchers, have produced findings indicating the benefit of religious involvement to health and well-being."[1]

Dr. Matthews mentions several studies that have to do with religious commitment and psychological health and well-being. For example, there is a 1983 study showing that religious commitment contributes to a better recovery of parents following the death of a child. The outcomes were particularly better among those whose religious convictions were strengthened during the mourning process. "These parents," Matthews writes, "had better psychological adjustment and fewer physical symptoms than those who did not experience strengthening of their religious beliefs during the bereavement period."[2]

There is also a 1993 study demonstrating the relationship between religious activity and fewer anxiety disorders. Researcher Harold Koenig looked at 2,969 individuals in conducting this study. He found that young and middle-aged individuals who attended church at least once a week "were significantly less likely to have anxiety-related disorders than those who did not attend church regularly. Among younger subjects, devotional activities such as prayer and Bible study were found to be linked with lower incidence of agoraphobia and other forms of anxiety."[3]

Finally, Matthews cites a study published in 1988 that measured the effects of religious involvement on well-being. This was a long-term study of 1,650 individuals over the course of 40 years. The individuals studied were asked to respond to surveys designed to rate their overall life satisfaction, specifically relating to marriage, work, and community. Matthews writes that respondents who attended church regularly "reported a significantly higher degree of overall life satisfaction, and those who reported strong religious beliefs were more likely to have happy marriages. Even after researchers applied controls to the data to account for influences of gender and income, church attendance and personal religious belief were still powerful factors in determining the happiness of these individuals."[4]

Matthews focuses upon the positive health outcomes of activities such as church attendance. This establishes a connection between spirituality and health. What about spirituality and actual healing? For that we turn to prayer. Larry Dossey, M.D., is one of the premier writers on this topic. In *Healing Words: The Power of Prayer and the Practice of Medicine*, Dr. Dossey states his reason for examining prayer and healing. "The most practical reason," he says, "is simply that, at least some of the time, *it works*. The evidence is simply overwhelming that prayer functions at a distance to change physical processes in a variety of organisms, from bacteria to humans."[5] In a later book, *Prayer Is Good Medicine*, Dr. Dossey notes his own amazement at finding more than 130 scientific studies on the general area of healing and prayer. "Over half of these experiments," Dossey writes, "strongly indicate that prayer works."[6]

What are some examples? Dossey cites a study by cardiologist Randolph Byrd designed to measure the impact of prayer upon patients committed to the coronary-care unit at San Francisco General Hospital. This was a randomized, double-blind experiment in which those admitted were randomly placed in one of two groups. One group was prayed for by home prayer groups while another was not. Each individual in the prayed-for group had between five and seven people praying for them. Dossey notes some interesting results from this experiment. The prayed-for group was "five times less likely to require antibiotics" and "three times less likely to develop pulmonary edema, a condition in which the lungs fill with fluid." No one in the prayed-for group required "endotracheal intubation, in which an artificial airway is inserted in the throat and attached to a mechanical ventilator, while twelve in the unremembered group required mechanical ventilatory support." Finally, although the difference was not statistically significant, fewer patients in the prayed-for group died.[7]

"If the technique being studied had been a new drug or a surgical procedure instead of prayer," Dossey concludes, "it would almost certainly have been heralded as some sort of 'breakthrough.'"[8]

Another group of experiments Dossey mentions measure the effects of prayer on nonhuman living systems. Dossey looks at these studies for a variety of reasons. They indicate the tangible results of prayer without creating difficulties related to human research. These studies raise fewer ethical questions (such as that of creating a group of patients who will *not* be prayed for), involve fewer variables, and are easier to interpret. Dr. Dossey found studies indicating the ability of prayer to retard the growth of fungus cultures, to impede the growth of cultures and bacteria, and to stimulate the growth of cultures and bacteria. Dossey cites studies of animals, demonstrating the ability of prayer to speed the healing of wounds in laboratory mice and in slowing the rate of adverse reactions in mice as the result of a change in diet.[9]

Dossey is so impressed with the effects of prayer on health that he believes it will eventually alter the practice of medicine. "The use of prayer," Dossey writes, "will become the standard in scientific medical practice in most medical communities."[10]

The third faith element in healing and wellness that we will look at is compassion. I consider compassion an element of spirituality because so much of the spiritual life teaches love for others. Love, as we saw in the last chapter, is ranked first among virtues by Saint Paul. Loving others and hoping the best for them is what compassion is all about. And, surprisingly, compassion can lead to healing.

Vegetarian and diet expert Dean Ornish, M.D., might appear to be an unlikely person to write on this topic. Dr. Ornish is mainly known for his advocacy of a low-fat diet program that is effective in reversing heart disease. His recent book, *Love and Survival*, however, focuses upon the emotional aspects of health. Ornish draws from several studies showing the negative consequences of such things as isolation, loneliness, and anger.

Among the studies that Dr. Ornish cites are those showing the impact of loving relationships on heart disease. One study of 119 men and 40 women at Yale showed that those who felt the most loved and supported "had substantially less blockage in the arteries of their hearts. The researchers found that feelings of being loved and emotionally supported were more important predictors of the severity of coronary artery blockages than was the number of relationships a person had. Equally important, this effect was independent of diet, smoking, exercise, cholesterol, family history (genetics), and other standard risk factors."[11]

Another study in Sweden found that women having the availability of deep emotional relationships had "less coronary artery blockage as measured by computer-analyzed coronary angiography."[12] Finally, researchers at Case Western Reserve University conducted a study of almost ten thousand married men who had no prior history of chest pain. Men who had high levels of such risk factors as high cholesterol, high blood pressure, and diabetes were over twenty times more likely to develop chest pain during the next five years. Most surprising was that those who answered yes to the question "Does your wife show you her love?" had "significantly less angina even when they had high levels of these risk factors. Men who had these risk factors but did not have a wife who showed her love had substantially increased angina [chest pain]—almost twice as much."[13]

Dr. Ornish's research in the area of relationships and heart disease, as well as the number of other studies he cites concerning the preventative and healing aspects of such practices as compassion, led him to make the following (rather startling) claim: "Love and intimacy," he writes, "are among the most powerful factors in health and illness, even though these ideas are largely ignored by the medical profession.... I am not aware of any other factor in medicine—not diet, not smoking, not exercise, not genetics, not drugs, not surgery—that has a greater impact on our quality of life, incidence of illness, and premature death from all causes."[14]

The possible spiritual element here is twofold. Spirituality promotes a love and compassion towards others. This, in turn, tends to create a desire for better relations with others, both at home and in the community. Ornish himself makes this connection through such statements as, "When the emotional heart and the *spiritual* heart begin to open, the physical heart often follows."[15] Ornish reaches the conclusion that anything that promotes intimacy "leads to greater joy and healing; anything that promotes isolation and loneliness leads to more suffering and illness."[16] A spiritual perspective is certainly something that will lead to greater intimacy and less isolation and loneliness.

Interestingly, Ornish makes a statement on love and intimacy that is similar to Dossey's statement that physicians who do not pray for their patients may someday be guilty of malpractice. "Love and intimacy," Ornish writes, "are at a root of what makes us sick and what makes us well, what causes sadness and what brings happiness, what makes us suffer and what leads to healing. If a new drug had the same impact, virtually every doctor in the country would be recommending it for their patients. It would be malpractice not to prescribe it."[17]

Worship, prayer, and compassion are nicely connected with healing and wellness. Each contributes in its own way to physical and emotional health. Each opens us to the miraculous. This is the message of a growing number of published studies by researchers and physicians.

Although there is a nice connection between faith and health, it is not always an easy one with which to live. We must also explore the connection between such emotions as anger and poor health. We are often pulled away from living faithfully by powerful emotions. In many respects, we become what we feel. I *am* the person who deeply enjoys the mountains, loves a woman named Karen, loves my children, and appreciates the feeling of accomplishment and peace after a good morning run.

Unfortunately, this is also true of our negative emotions. We are also people who get angry, who hate, and who take pleasure in our petty prejudices and jealousies. Such emotions have strong influences on us. L. Gregory Jones writes in his superb book on forgiveness that "many of us tend to define our own lives more by whom we hate than by whom or what we love. This can be both because of resentment and hatred that arise from our encounters with, and perhaps our suffering at the hands of, real enemies; but we must also confront our temptations to *create* enemies as a way of preserving our own distorted identities or our presumptions of power."[18]

To paraphrase Jones, we become our hatred of others. This is because the people we hate are woven into the fabric of the story of our lives. They are the people who have harmed us in some way. Because of this, it is extremely difficult to stop hating a person. In ceasing to hate someone it is as if, in a very deep sense, we give up something of our identity.

As hard as giving up hatred and anger are, they also go directly against the nice connection identified above. In fact, a growing body of evidence is accumulating to support an opposite connection; namely, between negative emotions and ill health. *Anger Kills*, written by Redford Williams, M.D., and Virginia Williams, Ph.D., is one of a number of books written on this connection. The title says it all. The Williams' cite studies showing that hostile people who are prone to cynicism, anger, and aggression are at higher risk of developing "life-threatening illness than are their less hostile counterparts." Such people tend to drive others away, and therefore fail to receive the healthful social support they need. Moreover, people given to anger are more likely to have a weakened immune system and will be more likely to engage in such risky behaviors as overeating, drinking excessively, and smoking.[19]

Such findings support the nice connection between faith and health. If behaviors associated with faith lead to good health, then we would expect that behaviors at odds with living within the Spirit would lead to poor health. This is exactly what the data show.

This is one reason why healers often emphasize the need to forgive. We've seen that who we hate defines who we are. Yet hate is at odds with the nice connection. The antidote to this is forgiveness. Forgiveness contributes to healing processes. It opens us up to the Spirit. Lack of forgiveness obstructs this, literally clogging our hearts and our spirits.

Let's turn briefly to two influential writers on healing to see the importance of love and forgiveness. Agnes Sanford was the wife of an Episcopalian priest who used her abilities to heal World War II veterans in U.S. hospitals. She became a prominent teacher and healer in the Spirit. Although she died more than two decades ago, she remains one of the most influential people in the area of spiritual-based healing. Her book, *The Healing Light*, is considered one of the classics in the field.

The Healing Light contains several references to the importance of forgiveness and love in healing. Ms. Sanford writes that in giving way to anger, the "protective and life-giving forces of the body are weakened so that one falls prey to germs and infections, to pain and weakness, to nervousness and ill temper, and to the spiritual dullness that results from the dimming of the life force."[20] She warns particularly of the human tendency to label one's anger a righteous anger. Anger we label as righteous, however correct we may feel it to be, is still poisonous to our systems. She recommends, following Jesus' sayings, that we avoid anger and direct our lives "towards paths of peace."[21] We are to practice forgiveness rather than revenge. Her method for doing this is disarmingly simple. When confronted with someone who is making you angry, simply send them love. See them as a child of God, forgiven as you are. This simple act makes a great deal of difference in people's lives.

Another influential writer on healing is Francis MacNutt. A former priest who now codirects Christian Healing Ministries in Clearwater, Florida, MacNutt is recognized as one of the leading experts in the field. MacNutt's recently revised landmark work, *Healing*, notes several studies showing that love and forgiveness have "an extraordinary effect upon our health. If we can only learn to fulfill Jesus' great commandment to love God and one another, our physical health, as well as our spiritual, would flourish!"[22] MacNutt is consistent with Agnes Sanford in noting that hatred causes toxicity to build in our bodies, while forgiveness produces amazing healing results.

The problem with just taking Sanford's and MacNutt's statements at face value, however, is that forgiveness is just not easy. We hate the people we do for a reason.

Usually these are people who have harmed us in some way or people we feel threatened by. Perhaps they are too different from us, and we dislike them for it. Perhaps they have traits that remind us of ourselves, our own negative traits, and that, too, is threatening.

Sometimes hatred and anger are over very serious matters. Victims of rape, child abuse, domestic abuse, and other forms of violence have deep reasons for their anger. It is unreal, and even damaging, to suggest that such victims merely forgive the people who have harmed them. A term that is sometimes used for this is "cheap grace." Proponents of cheap grace would simply tell a victim of domestic violence, for example, to forgive their abusive spouse and pray for the spouse's forgiveness.

A more realistic and correct view is to see forgiveness as a craft. It is something we can learn over time, forgiving the smaller hurts and then finding our way to forgive the larger ones. Within the craft is also the need to remove oneself from threatening situations, for trying to forgive someone in situations of violence and oppression is both difficult and unrealistic. Remembering the Book of Ecclesiastes, there are times for all things. Suffering from abuse indicates a time to leave and seek support and shelter. Then one can take on what will be the long-term task of finding forgiveness and wholeness while exercising the wisdom to try to remain in safety.

The ideas behind the craft of forgiveness are well explained by Jones' *Embodying Forgiveness*. Important here again is that forgiveness, even for nonviolent offenses, takes time. Jones recounts one of C. S. Lewis' experiences. Lewis wrote in one of his letters that during prayer one day he discovered that "I had really forgiven someone I had been trying to forgive for over 30 years." Jones notes that 30 years "might seem an extraordinarily long time to some, unrealistic to others, and to yet others— particularly those who have unjustly suffered something, or some things, of great magnitude—it might seem unexpectedly brief."[23]

Our task as Christians is to find ways toward forgiveness. This means seeking pathways of love as opposed to pathways of vengeance. Unfortunately, this goes against our nature, to say nothing of dominant views on retribution and payment for injustice. We need, as Jones writes, to find ways of embodying the craft of forgiveness. The "struggle" to do this means engaging in attitudes and behaviors from "learning to live with memories of the past to coping with feelings of resentment and desires for vengeance, to loving our enemies, and to becoming proficient exemplars of holiness through habits and practices of forgiveness and reconciliation."[24]

This all takes time. Linking this to writings on healing, however, provides hope. For here we see we have help. Left to our own devices, we might never be able to forgive and live within the glow of the nice connection. The Holy Spirit is there with us, among us, and in us. In praying for the healing of the Holy Spirit, we find ways to cope with our anger towards those who have wronged us or whom we dislike. We also find ways to experience our own forgiveness. Such simple methods as that provided by Agnes Sanford earlier (we will look at more such methods later) are excellent means of inviting the Holy Spirit in as a healing force in our lives and in the lives of others. Make no mistake about it, though, you will have to pray long and hard at forgiveness when it comes to certain matters, and it may take years to experience the grace of forgiveness. We are, after all, human. Still, it is a task we are called upon to undertake, a race we need to run.

There is much to suggest a nice connection between faith and healing. Equally, there is much to suggest a connection between the works of the flesh and illness and disease. Some, like Amanda at the beginning of this chapter, live as healers within the miraculous side of the nice connection. We, too, have the ability to step into this realm. In doing so, we must not succumb to the works that Saint Paul describes as quarrels, dissensions, envy, and anger (Gal 5:20–21). We must, with the help of the Holy Spirit, find our way to forgiveness and love. This is a way to living within the healing of the nice connection.

Exercise 3:
Practicing the Craft of Forgiveness

Anger and the failure to forgive often have toxic effects on our bodies. They are the negative side of the nice connection. To counter these emotions, begin to practice the craft of forgiveness. Start slowly by practicing forgiveness with respect to minor irritations. Practice this forgiveness over the course of the next few days and then record

what you experience. Then think about how you
can expand this practice to people whom you may
find more difficult to forgive.

The Healing Encounter

ONLY FOUR OTHER PEOPLE sat in the small library of the church. They are part of a healing group that meets there once a month. Each member discussed how they had experienced healing in their lives. One woman talked about her cancer, now in remission for several years. Another spoke of a healing he had witnessed at a local church service and of the electric shock he felt when the healer at the service touched him. A third sought healing for her daughter who was going through a divorce. At the end of the discussion the fourth person, a priest, anointed each one of us in succession. We all joined the priest in placing our hands upon the person being anointed, praying for healing to continue in their lives.

I must admit that I was not entirely comfortable there. The idea of this kind of service makes me a little nervous. I live, after all, in the South, famous for snake handlers and faith-healing charlatans. Still, there was an enormous sense of peace in the room. I have no doubt that real healing had taken place in the lives of those present.

Such experiences are out there, ready to be had. From a Christian perspective, we can open our hearts and minds to these experiences. Recall in the last chapter that we discussed the importance of faith to healing. Faith is certainly something that we can enjoy and deepen through practice. Faith opens us up to experiencing the presence of God. This, in turn, grants us the experience of all manner of things, among them healing. We can become witnesses to healing as well as people who experience it ourselves. This is one of the many qualities of being a Christian.

In this chapter we deepen our understanding of healing. We do so by looking at it as part of our encounter with suffering. In this we see the good and bad elements associated with healing. Healing is certainly good, for we all want to see ourselves and our loved ones healed of their afflictions. Yet a complete view of healing also requires that we look at suffering. We must understand this suffering, understand what it means from a Christian perspective, before we can truly appreciate the healing mission of Christ. We will do this by looking at real encounters with suffering so that we may see the seeds of healing contained therein. We will also take a hard look at the place of suffering and healing in our faith.

Since Elizabeth Kubler-Ross' groundbreaking study, *Death and Dying*, much has been written about the process of dealing with terminal illness. The encounter with serious illness often leads to a predictable process within the sufferer. People deny the illness and get angry about it before moving to an acceptance of their situation. People can get stuck, though, and not get to the stage of acceptance and action. They may end up depressed or bitter and be unable to find a way to move out of such a state. Similarly, they may stay in denial and refuse to deal with their situation in a conscious way. Some become passive participants in a medical system that is more than willing to tell them exactly what to do.

A recent study of those infected with HIV (human immunodeficiency virus) illustrates the process involved in the encounter with a serious condition. Psychiatrist Robert Klitzman's *Being Positive* is an insightful account based upon the experiences of HIV-infected individuals. These people come from all walks of life, though many became infected either through engaging in risky sexual behavior or as a result of being intravenous drug users.

Reminiscent of Kubler-Ross, Klitzman finds that HIV infection engenders a process that he describes as a journey. The journey has both medical and emotional aspects to it. He writes:

> *HIV infection constitutes a journey for infected individuals, who experience it in different ways. The point at which they first begin to confront the infection varies, and disbelief, alienation, and delay commonly occur. A long series of events follows, including lab tests and symptoms—visible and unseen, specific to HIV, diagnostic of AIDS, and requiring medication. A series of losses also ensues—of function, mind, future, socioeconomic status, and friends. These transitions and stresses produce a roller-coaster effect as individuals struggle to find ways to cope.*[1]

Dr. Klitzman finds six forms of response among the HIV-positive individuals he followed. The first is what he calls immersion into HIV-land, or becoming involved in the HIV "community" and receiving information and support there. Three other responses are appealing to higher powers, work and volunteerism, and increasing ties with family. These first four responses provide important sources of meaning to the sufferer and help to buffer "the depression, anxiety, and 'existential angst' resulting from the infection." The fifth response, that of minimizing the disease, can alleviate psychological problems, though "other problems of health behavior may result." The final response, substance abuse, "may numb feelings fleetingly but contribute[s] in the long run to other difficulties."[2]

This categorization of responses is helpful in understanding effective and ineffective responses to the encounter with HIV and with illness in general. The four positive responses that Klitzman uncovers involve seeking support from the similarly afflicted and from friends and family, as well as connecting with a higher Power (spirituality) and volunteering to help others. On the ineffective side, sufferers may either go into denial or engage in such destructive behaviors as substance abuse. It is possible, too, that a person may not choose any of the above responses. In the absence of any of these modes of response, Klitzman writes that "depression and despair as well as suicidal thoughts commonly occur."[3]

There are two other findings of Klitzman's study that are worth mentioning. The first is that of the possibilities that HIV infection presents to sufferers. Some of those mentioned in Klitzman's book actually saw HIV as a chance to straighten up lives that involved practices destructive to themselves and to others. I am speaking here of those involved in intravenous drug use and sharing needles, as well as those engaged in promiscuous and risky sexual practices. The possibility presented is that of getting one's life in order and, in effect, becoming whole. As one infected, former intravenous drug user said: "Sometimes now when I wake up in the morning I feel like a normal person. HIV has been a blessing in disguise—a second chance."[4]

The second aspect of the study is that of the unique place of spirituality in helping some HIV-infected individuals. Klitzman found that spirituality helped individuals deal with the reasons for their illness (and any feelings of culpability they may have) as well as providing a more positive view of the future. Thus spirituality helps to address "issues of responsibility and fate" and offers "hope."[5] This may well be why those who don't rely upon religious or spiritual support "tend to be more depressed."[6]

Dr. Klitzman's work with HIV-infected individuals helps us to put a real face on the encounter with illness. The encounter, of course, is a harsh one. It is certainly understandable to see people engage in self-pity, anger, denial, and any number of other "negative" emotions. The encounter also has a positive side. It may cause people to reach out to others and to find their faith. These activities may lead to either tangible, physical healing or to deeper, spiritual healing.

Before discussing in more detail the healing side of

illness, I want to mention one other moving account of an individual's encounter with serious disease. Actually, this is less of one person's encounter with illness than that of a husband and wife. Sidney Winawer first suspected his wife, Andrea, might be seriously ill when they came home one evening from a New Year's Eve party. She had a stomachache, but it did not sound as if it were a run-of-the-mill type pain. A cancer specialist at the prestigious Sloane-Kettering Cancer Center in New York, Dr. Winawer knew when to be suspicious.

Dr. Winawer presents a moving account of he and Andrea's ordeal with cancer in his book, *Healing Lessons*. As it turns out, Winawer's suspicions about his wife's illness were confirmed. She was diagnosed with stomach cancer and told that she only had a few months to live. She was encouraged to begin a radical program of chemotherapy. Andrea resisted, choosing instead to look into more experimental methods.

As is true of many who tend to do better (that is, live longer) in the face of serious illness, Andrea became an active participant in the healthcare decisions that involved her.[7] Although she died three years after being diagnosed, and eventually did go through the radical program, she lived several months beyond her initial diagnosis and even enjoyed a fairly long period of good health.

Winawer attributes his wife's extended longevity to her willingness to explore unconventional treatments. Along with this was her willingness to seek out psychological and spiritual healing. Andrea continued to see a therapist during this time, as well as to practice methods recommended by such writers as Lawrence LeShan, Louise Hayes, and Norman Cousins.

Ironically, this "complementary" approach to Andrea's treatment was not something Dr. Winawer had been used to recommending for his own patients. During a period when Andrea's health was improving, Winawer returned to practice at Sloane-Kettering. He found himself recommending books and practices on meditation to cancer patients, as well as listening more to the emotional side of what the person was experiencing.

Sidney and Andrea drew heavily from spirituality in dealing with their encounter with her disease. They leaned upon the Jewish heritage that they shared and began reading the Bible. Dr. Winawer began to see that faith can be strong medicine, "a medicine of which we doctors should be more aware and encourage whenever possible."[8] Far from leading to a rejection of God due to the ultimate death of Andrea, both were better able to deal with her worsening condition as a result of their growing spirituality. This led to yet another poignant realization on the part of Winawer the physician. "Physicians," he writes, "have always been trained to keep people alive. Anything else is failure. We as doctors and the medical establishment have to get over that. Of course survival is monumental, but death is not a failure."[9]

Prayer became central to the spirituality that Sidney and Andrea practiced during her illness. It enabled them to let go of the idea that they had to bear this by themselves. There was something else to lean upon. Dr. Winawer puts it this way:

*The appeal of praying was exactly what I remem-
bered from my childhood. It was an act of surrender,
of giving up authority, of admitting you can't do it all
by yourself. This was the opposite of the activism that
doctors were used to. We always think we can solve
the problem, but sometimes we can't. Praying was a
way of holding in balance the wish to heal and the
need to admit that sometimes things are out of our
hands.*[10]

We learn from both Klitzman's study of HIV-infected
individuals and Dr. Winawer's account of how a couple
deals with cancer. In these encounters with illness, we see
the importance of taking an active part in dealing with a
serious illness. The tangible physical and emotional benefit of drawing upon spirituality and prayer in dealing
with disease is also evident. We must also note, however,
that these are not stories of miraculous healing. Nowhere
does Dr. Klitzman indicate that prayer or spiritual practices of any sort changed the HIV-positive status of any
of the individuals he followed. And Andrea Winawer
eventually died.

This brings me to the point of making an important
distinction in using such a practice as prayer to cope with
a serious illness. In short, prayer may not "work" if what
you are looking for is total physical recovery. There is a
deeper sense, though, where it does. I will speak, then, of
the difference between healing and *healing*, using the italicized word to distinguish the two senses. Healing is when
a person's condition is significantly reversed. That is, the

cancer is eradicated, the debilitating muscular disease cured, or the mental disorder ended. Such things really do happen as a result of prayer. *Healing* is when something different happens. It is when the surrendering takes place that Dr. Winawer discussed. In this surrendering is a deeper wholeness. It is the realization that, in some sense, we are part of a larger Presence, and that we can experience this Presence now. This experience does not depend upon our physical health, nor does it depend upon our longevity. It is a realization of the eternity that we can experience now, and of the continuing and greater experience of eternity that awaits us in turning to God.

The encounter with illness may be a healing one and a *healing* one. Further, there is something about this encounter that can take us very deep indeed into the experience of God. To illustrate this point, let's compare the notion of suffering in Christianity with that in Buddhism. This comparison is not meant to prove one religion as better than the other, but rather to highlight something about the Christian tradition which I embrace.

For years I have been intrigued by the Buddhist approach to suffering. This approach goes to the very heart of their beliefs. The Buddha is said to have uttered what are known as the four noble truths. There are many different translations of these truths. The one I will use is a paraphrase of the interpretation given by Zen Buddhist and psychotherapist David Brazier in his recent book, *The Feeling Buddha*. Roughly, the four noble truths are these:

1. Life is suffering and affliction.
2. This situation gives rise to such feelings as greed, passion, and anger.
3. To keep from being overcome with such feelings, refuse to dwell upon them. Thinking must be contained or restricted in order to do this.
4. To further this process, and attain enlightenment, follow the eightfold path. That is right view, right thought, right speech, right action, right livelihood, right effort, right mindfulness, and right awakening.[11]

What intrigues me about the above is that it is effective in dealing with the problem of suffering. I have been able to use it myself to understand when I am suffering about something. For example, I now see many of my work-related concerns as being the result of a desire to be viewed positively by everyone. Using the above allows me to see the problem in a new light. If I can contain this desire, which is really both egotistical and irrational, then I can ease my suffering. In this, the four noble truths fit nicely with methods found both in Cognitive Psychology[12] and the Psychology of Mind.[13] Here the idea is to question irrational assumptions about your view of the world (Cognitive Psychology) or to look at your thinking and replace it with more positive thoughts (Psychology of Mind).

The four noble truths may also be applied to physical suffering to produce some of the same outcomes as described by Winawer and Klitzman. If people have cancer, say, then they can see their suffering as the result of their anger over the situation and their desire for a long, healthy life. To ease this suffering, they may contain this desire and replace it with a more realistic appraisal of the situation. Anger, of course, accomplishes nothing. "Right thinking" frees the sufferer from the negative thinking that really ends up getting in the way of positive action. They may then engage in the four response modes that Klitzman mentions, these being seeking community, turning to spirituality, volunteerism, and finding family support. At a minimum, an application of the four noble truths could well get someone past the initial anger and depression that goes along with an initial diagnosis of terminal illness.

What troubled me for some time was my failure to find a similar approach to suffering from Christianity. Often when someone we know is suffering, it is difficult to find, from a Christian standpoint, the brief and effective message that a sufferer might be looking for. I am reminded of a minister I knew named Tom who attended the funeral of a four-year-old girl who was killed in a tragic accident. The message from the minister presiding at the funeral was that God didn't have enough four-year-olds in heaven. The idea that God would so populate heaven, and that this should be seen as words of comfort to an ailing family, made Tom literally sick to his stomach.

Looking at such issues as suffering, healing, and *healing*, however, it is essential that we see that something different is going on in Christianity than in Buddhism. Both Christianity and Buddhism agree that there is a great deal of suffering in the world. In Buddhism this is evident from the four noble truths. In Christianity, as well as Judaism, we also see an acknowledgment of suffering. This begins with Genesis, where in the story of Adam and Eve we find the explanation of suffering found by their eating from the fruit of the tree of life. Genesis 3:14–19 describes the life of suffering that humans must now tolerate as a result of this action.

Suffering finds its way into a great deal of the rest of the Scriptures. We find in such books as Job and the Psalms discussions of the suffering that is our lot as human beings. Psalm 44, for example, is a particularly angry cry to God. Here the psalmist makes such statements as "You have rejected and abased us," "You have made us the taunt of our neighbors," and "All day long my disgrace is before me" (9, 13, and 15).

What is the Christian response to this suffering? Similar to Buddhism, the Christian response focuses directly upon the situation of suffering. Christ is, after all, sent to suffer and die for our sins. One of the most known and repeated verses from the Bible is John 3:16: "For God so loved the world that he gave his only Son, so that everyone who believes in him may not perish but have eternal life." The reason for this is stated in the next verse. Here it says, "Indeed, God did not send the Son into the world to condemn the world, but in order that the world might be saved through him."

It might be tempting simply to stop there. Going back to the Adam and Eve story, we would simply say that humans suffer due to original sin, and that Christ died to take away these sins. The problem is that Christ's death did not take away our earthly suffering. Continuing to read the gospels and the rest of the New Testament, we see that suffering, particularly in the form of religious persecution, continued. The apostles had to deal with difficult situations, with illness, and with hardships of every kind.

Suffering did not end with Christ's death and Resurrection. What does take place, however, is a different view of suffering. Suffering allows us to identify with Christ and thereby to become participants in redemption. Thus in Romans it says that we suffer with Christ so that we "may also be glorified with him" (8:17). The first epistle of Peter also instructs readers to rejoice in the sharing of Christ's sufferings so that they may be glad and shout for joy "when his glory is revealed" (4:13).

Finally, returning to Romans, we get a statement that is as close as any to a type of methodology that can be applied to suffering, just as the four noble truths may be applied. Here Saint Paul writes that suffering "produces endurance, and endurance produces character, and character produces hope, and hope does not disappoint us, because God's love has been poured into our hearts through the Holy Spirit that has been given to us" (5:3–5). In suffering, then, we have the opportunity to reach down within ourselves and find both character and hope. The hope that we find is particularly powerful, for it is redemptive hope. It is the hope that is given to us by the Holy Spirit, and one which leans heavily upon the realization that Christ's love for us will, in the end, not let us down.

I think that Saint Paul's characterization of suffering is made more complete by combining it with Saint Peter's notion that suffering allows us to participate with Christ. Combining these notions, we get the idea that suffering not only enables us to look within ourselves to find character and hope but also allows us to identify and participate with Christ in redemption. My suffering, in short, is the vehicle through which I am able to see Christ's enormous sacrifice for me, and through which I understand and experience grace in a deeper way. Importantly, it is also a means for me to be a window through which others may look and see the reality of their own redemption through Christ. Any suffering we experience may be used as a means to bring others to Christ. This is eloquently put in Hebrews 13, where Jesus is described as being sacrificed "outside the city gate in order to sanctify the people of his own blood." We, too, can go outside of the city gates of ourselves and of our own suffering, so that we offer a "sacrifice of praise to God, that is, the fruit of the lips that confess his name" (13:12–15).

Is there a simple Christian method to understand and cope with the suffering? There is. It may be stated as follows:

1. Human suffering is part of the natural order of things.
2. In suffering we find the opportunity to develop character and endurance and to experience more deeply the hope that is ours through Christ.
3. Suffering also allows us to identify with Christ's redemption of us.

4. We can participate in this redemptive effort through offering our suffering as a sacrifice of praise.

Interestingly, the above is remarkably consistent with Klitzman's findings. It addresses the positive responses to HIV infection in ways that perhaps Buddhism does not. Reaching out to fellow sufferers and actively engaging in efforts to find treatments and cures is part of what endurance is all about. Volunteerism and spirituality are also deeply ingrained in the above, for through these activities we find hope and meaning, sentiments echoed within those who Klitzman found practiced positive means of dealing with their infection. The method above is also consistent with Klitzman's finding that spirituality provided hope and meaning to the infected, for the above method provides quite a deep sense of meaning indeed.

Importantly, this view of suffering also shows what it is not. Although suffering may be a means for us to glorify God and to participate in the redemption of the world, it is not something we should seek out. Nor is it something we should passively accept. Our response to suffering is an active one. It is active in two senses, for, as we saw in James, Scripture tells us if we are ill to seek healing. The message from the above gives us another means to be active in our suffering. If we do not find the physical healing we seek, we can use our afflictions as a base from which to help others. In that, too, there is healing.

Certainly, then, the encounter with illness is one that reveals a great deal of suffering. Returning to the small group of people I described at the beginning of this chapter, there had obviously been some real suffering among them. They had faced sickness and death, and had suffered because of it. At the same time, the encounter had a positive face to it. There was healing that had taken place in their lives. More importantly, though, was that an opportunity for *healing* had taken place. That is, a healing of the soul. For illness can be a part of the healing power of sanctification found in Christ. Though the journey is difficult, there is always a deeper hope. That hope is something that we all have an opportunity in which to participate. For though we will all suffer, every one of us, we can, through faith, experience and participate in the redemptive power of grace.

Exercise 4: Participation

> Look at whatever you may be suffering from. In addition to praying and seeking whatever medical, psychological, or emotional help you may need, list how you can participate in the redemption of others through your ailment. Are there some unique avenues open to you that allow you to help others and to be a blessing to them? List these, and then select at least one to pursue. Pray for the help of the Holy Spirit as you pursue this course.

Prayer-Centered Healing

RECENTLY I ASKED writer and spiritual healing advocate King Oehmig what common characteristics he saw in people who experienced a spiritual-based healing. "They prayed their butts off," he said without hesitating.

Praying, and praying often, is a piece of advice given by many writing about healing. "Pray without ceasing," we are told in 1 Thessalonians 5:17. This advice easily applies to those praying for healing.

Let's start this discussion of prayer-centered healing from what may seem an unlikely source. Quantum physics provides us with an interesting possibility that, whether true or not, says something about the choices we make as human beings. Quantum physics is a modern branch of physics deriving from the formulations of the most noteworthy physicists of our time, among them Werner Heisenberg, Niels Bohr, and Erwin Schrödinger. This branch of physics is often concerned with uncertainty and possibility. In fact, one of the ideas upon which it is based is the uncertainty principle. This principle springs from our inability to obtain truly objective information about the world. The very act of attempting to measure something such as an electron changes the electron itself. This is because of the influence of the measuring equipment upon the electron. "The process of observation itself," writes Richard P. Brennan in the *Dictionary of Scientific Literacy*, "changes the object being studied."[1] This situation creates formidable obstacles to human knowledge. "Since humankind can only perceive reality through the medium of the senses," Brennan continues, "there is a limit to what humanity can know."[2]

One possibility that quantum physics considers is that of parallel universes. This is based in part upon the uncertainty principle and the influence we as perceivers, interpreters, and actors have upon the world. When faced with a particular situation, we may choose to act in one of a number of ways. If we act one way, then a particular set of events will occur. If we act in another way, then an entirely different set of events will occur. The idea is that the choices we make have an influence upon the world, just as our observation has an influence upon that which is observed.

Please think very carefully about this. The way you react to this world has a direct impact upon it. If something happens to you, if someone harms you in some way, and you choose the path of hatred and vengeance as opposed to a prayerful and loving response, then certain things will happen. That is a fact.

There is a useful metaphor to help us take this further. Physicist Fred Alan Wolff's book, *Taking the Quantum*

Leap, offers some surprisingly practical advice about living based upon his work in quantum physics. He invites us to look at parallel universes as if they are branches on a tree.

> *Keep choosing which branch you want to sample life on. Remember that you are on all branches that you can exist on. It's up to you which branch you happen to be sampling now. And since joy for all people is a desire, eventually all will be joyful if that is the branch we all wish to be aware on.*
>
> *Think of the branches as branches of a tree and of the sense of self you now feel as the sap or lifeblood of the tree. Feed the good branches.*[3]

Feed the good branches. The tree metaphor is a powerful one. It is useful even if there are no parallel universes. Simply think of your life as you would like it to be from this point forward. Do you want to be more joyous? Do you want it to be a healed, whole life? Would you like to be a healer, one who touches and renews others through love? Start making the choices that lead to experiencing life on that branch.

Is there some help we can find in making such choices? This is another extremely important question. Since we are humans and prone to habits and weaknesses, seemingly easy changes are often difficult to implement. I may say that I will make the choices necessary to become a less angry person and that I will always act for the benefit of others, but my actually doing these things is much more difficult. We all have deep-seated emotions and ways of being that we carry around. When faced with a situation when there is a chance to choose a more joyous response, our very natures often get in the way. We choose out of anger rather than love, and the universe responds accordingly.

That is why we need help. The Holy Spirit is our guide here. In the Spirit we are able to move past our natures in miraculous ways. In the Spirit we find a healing grace that allows us to make joyous choices. To receive this help, we need to have a method for tapping into the Spirit. Prayer is that method. Prayer is the means of finding the healing gifts of the Spirit. Opening our hearts to God pushes us to those branches where the universe responds to petition and intercession. This is the place where healing takes place in you and in those for whom you pray.

In bringing this out I return to an author mentioned in the previous chapter. Agnes Sanford is helpful because of the centrality of prayer to her healing ministry. One of her main concerns is with explaining the method and power of the prayer of faith. This is the same phrase we find in James' epistle, "The prayer of faith will save the sick, and the Lord will raise them up" (5:15). In terms of the power of this prayer, Sanford's words are surprisingly consistent with those of Wolff. It is not only our prayers but also our actions in line with our prayers that create a better, more joyous, and more healed life.

I have already mentioned something of Sanford's background. Notable is that she came from a tradition that did not emphasize a connection between faith and healing. Her autobiography, *Sealed Orders*, recounts a conversation she had as a child with her mother. After reciting the passage in John 14:12 in which it says that those believing in Jesus shall do the works that he does, she asked her mother why they weren't able to do such works. "Because the age of miracles is past," her mother said. "This is a new dispensation."

Looking back as an adult, Sanford writes that "God bless them, for they were as good and as completely consecrated people as one could find. They were not consciously lying. But they had been misinformed. The age of miracles is not past. This is not theory, but is a matter of absolute knowledge; I have seen miracles."[4]

Ms. Sanford began her own healing ministry when, as a young mother married to a minister and living in the United States, one of her children remained ill for many weeks with abscessed ears. One day a minister came to visit her. Upon hearing that her child was ill, he told Sanford that he would go up and pray for the child. She was skeptical, thinking that she had already prayed. She told the young man that she didn't think he could do any good since the baby was so young and wouldn't understand what was happening.

The minister said that wouldn't matter and went upstairs to the baby's room with Sanford following close behind. Sanford watched as the man put his hands on the baby's ears and said, "Now you close your eyes and go to sleep. I'm going to ask God to come into your ears and make them well, and when you wake up you'll be all right." The minister closed his prayer by saying, "We thank you, Heavenly Father, because we know that this is being done. Amen"[5]

To Sanford's surprise, the baby instantly appeared healthier. The baby fell asleep, and when he awoke, all was well.

This experience caused Sanford to reconsider the attitude towards faith and healing that she had inherited from her parents. She began to explore healing and soon became a powerful healer, with prayer-centered healing as the primary means used in her approach. Particularly helpful is that she gives us a method for the prayer of faith. This prayer is exemplified by the actions of the young minister above.

In *Healing Gifts of the Spirit* Sanford gives another example of the method and power of the prayer of faith. Once when traveling on a train between Washington, D.C., and Philadelphia she noticed that she became inexplicably alert after settling into her seat. This was odd since she had spent the entire day lecturing and performing healing services, and should have been exhausted. She became so agitated that she decided to pray.

The train pulled into its Baltimore stop and then started once more upon its way. Suddenly there was a loud crash as a large stone from a steep embankment shattered a window close to Sanford. Glass was everywhere. Sanford immediately became concerned about the young man in front of her whom she could no longer see. She found him drooped over the end of his seat with blood spilling from his forehead. "Clearly," Sanford writes, "I had been planted there by the Lord to be the channel of healing for this man."

As everyone was rushing about making arrangements for an ambulance to pick up the young man at the next stop, Sanford reached forward and placed her hands beneath the man's head. If anyone asked what she was doing, she simply said that she was supporting his head. "But while supporting it I continued silently to pray the prayer of faith," she writes, "asking for God's healing light to come into him and to completely and immediately heal the wound. I then gave thanks that it was so, expressing that thanks both in the word 'Amen' and in the English translation of it which is 'So it is.' And I lent to the prayer the power of my imagination, seeing the wound healed."[6]

In less than ten minutes the man regained consciousness and wanted to know what all the fuss was about. When told he was going to be taken out to an ambulance at the next stop, he said he was fine and didn't need one. When the train stopped and they took him anyway, still protesting, Sanford got a glimpse of his forehead as he turned around. The cut was now only a "thin white line, like a scar some three weeks old. And he walked down the aisle tall and straight, quite alone and still protesting."[7]

Both this story and the one of the young minister healing Sanford's child show the method and the power of the prayer of faith. In her books *The Healing Light* and *The Healing Gifts of the Spirit* Sanford discusses the method of this prayer. *The Healing Gifts of the Spirit* describes the method of this prayer as follows:

1. Choose which symptom or weakness you wish to pray about first and do not try to pray for all of them at once.
2. Form your prayer in words that suggest to the body the healed condition and not the continuing trouble.
3. Make, in the imagination, a picture of the thing that you purpose in prayer. Hold this picture in mind as much as possible, but lightly, as one plays a game.
4. Give thanks to God that His power is entering and is working toward wholeness in the body in all ways best according to His will.[8]

Although sometimes stated differently by Sanford, the approach is basically the same as outlined above. The idea is to recognize the power of God, take that power within you, identify that which you wish to see healed, pray as if the condition were being healed, and give thanks for the healing. This method worked for Sanford on numerous occasions.

There are certain aspects of Sanford's work on prayer and healing that need to be highlighted. Sanford not only talks about the need to recognize the reality of God, but to become deeply aware of his presence. "We receive God, in other words, by forgetting ourselves and thinking about Him. Therefore we begin our prayer not by clamoring for this and that before we have even reached His presence, but by thinking about Him in the way that makes Him most real to us."[9] The need here is not to begin immediately to petition God for healing, however strong that temptation may be. Slow down and experience God first. Experience God's wonderful presence and open up to it, allowing yourself to become totally immersed within it. Then, when you are so deeply immersed that you have almost forgotten yourself entirely, pray for the healing you seek.

Sanford also advises us to have prayer objectives in mind, to keep these limited and focused, and to keep praying until something happens. "Chose only a few objects for prayer at a time," she writes. Keep them "plain, concise, and concrete."[10] If the healing sought does not occur right away, keep praying until it does. "How long should we continue praying for healing?" she asks. "Until the healing is accomplished."[11] We may pray once or twice a day or, if necessary, pray continuously. The point is to keep praying.

Another key element in healing is to understand the importance of forgiveness. Although we touched on this in the last chapter, it is worthwhile looking at this in more detail. Sanford speaks a great deal not only about our need to forgive others but also about our need to feel forgiven. In her experience she found that many people were not healed until they felt forgiven. The experience of a lack of forgiveness is often something of an illness itself. She finds that as we practice the work of forgiveness we discover that "healing and forgiveness are one."[12]

As far as failure to forgive others is concerned, the problem is that such failures align us with the negative forces in the universe, those forces that are not in sync with God. Sanford warns of the need not to dwell on anger and to forgive adversaries quickly so as not to succumb to the cancer of hatred. "We would be wise to take the wrath-provoking words and acts of other people as assignments from God, as spiritual exercises, or as helpful hints along the way of life rather than as excuses for anger."[13]

Sanford offers a very practical and forceful method of forgiving others. "The first step in forgiveness," she writes, "is the overcoming of resentment, that is, learning to like someone whom one has not liked before. The second step, which should follow spontaneously and naturally upon the first, is the recreation of the forgiven one by love."[14] Sanford says that we should first look to our own resentment and attempt to overcome that. The second step, which follows from the first, is to change the way we look at the person whom we need to forgive, and to put this changed way into practice. "Having forgiven someone," she writes, "we do not see his faults any more. Instead of that, we see his virtues, creating in our minds by faith the exact opposite of the traits that has annoyed us in this person, and projecting them by faith into reality. These good and happy traits will often rise to the surface and be manifest, as if they had been there all the time only awaiting the touch of love to bring them forth."[15]

It does no good to forgive someone in your mind and not act upon that forgiveness. You must act as if you forgive that person, and see them as someone who is loved by God. In doing this, you must also look for the good traits they possess, and act so that more of these traits are displayed. While this will not work in every instance where anger and other negative emotions are involved, it will work in many.

Sanford even goes so far as to suggest that we look for instances where we can practice the forgiveness of others. Once we identify someone towards whom we are not well disposed, she suggests that we change the relationship not by prayer and thought, but by action. "*Do something, not only to show kindness to the other person but, more importantly, to indicate to your own subconscious that it is your will to love.*"[16]

The results of this approach can be quite amazing. A few years ago, for example, I was asked to teach a short management class after work. I reluctantly agreed to do it as a favor to the friend who had asked. On the first day I asked class members to give me their name and what they expected to get from the experience. When it came the turn of an older gentlemen in the class he gave his name and said simply that he doubted whether I had anything at all to teach him and that he was only coming out of curiosity more than anything else. I noted a tone of cynicism and disdain in his voice.

His statement bothered me throughout the rest of the hour. I took it as a direct affront to me. Here I was, volunteering to do this class, taking good time out of my day, just to hear this sort of thing. I didn't have to do this, and he didn't have to attend. I wished that he would just not be there the next time the class met.

As it turned out, he kept coming. Rather than allowing my resentment to get in the way of our relationship, I decided to pray and act out of forgiveness. My action was to act as if he hadn't meant his words the way they sounded. Rather than avoid him, I sought him out and looked for his good qualities.

What I found was a man with a great deal of knowledge and insight. He is now a good friend. While occasionally gruff, he is also remarkably kind and concerned about others. He is someone whose opinion I truly respect, for he is one of those rare people who is not afraid to speak his mind. Had I acted upon my initial resentment I would have missed a real opportunity.

Putting Sanford's thoughts together we see the prayer of faith at the core of her practice. It is a very simple and direct method for healing involving total immersion into God, knowing what to pray for and asking for it, seeing what you want to happen, and giving thanks to God for the healing being brought about.

Beyond Sanford's prayer-centered approach to healing is also a prayer-centered approach to life. That is, living a life that is clearly fuller in the Spirit. Chief among the qualities of this life is forgiveness. In forgiveness we open ourselves up to a greater extent to the love of God. This love has a direct impact upon healing. Anger, hatred, and vengeance, on the other hand, close us from this love, and we would do well to learn ways to avoid these.

I do not want to leave the impression from the above that Sanford is the final word on healing and prayer. What she gives us is a simple and direct approach to healing, one that recognizes not only the importance of praying, but on acting as well. There are many other types of prayer that are helpful in healing. Some are particularly effective in dealing with particular life situations. Bridget Meehan's book, *The Healing Power of Prayer*, provides several examples of other types of healing prayer. Among them are the Healing of Memories prayer, the Forgiveness Prayer, Centering Prayer, Relaxation Prayer, and the Prayer of the Sufferer.[17] Similar to Sanford, Meehan calls for action, faith, and patient understanding in approaching God through healing prayer. "As instruments of God," she writes, "we are called to do more than pray for others." We need to perform such prayer-centered actions as listening and exhibiting understanding towards sufferers. Additionally, she advises us to pray with faith, remembering that healing is a process "that happens in God's time and according to divine plan."[18]

One final addition to make regarding prayer and healing is to see the seemingly contradictory notions of consistency and surprise contained within a prayer-centered approach. Consistency is important because we need to establish a closer relationship to God. This requires practice. As we move through our daily lives, it is vital that we find moments to reach to God and that we expand these moments so that they are woven into the fabric of our lives. Without doing this, we succumb to the pushes and pulls of the world far too easily.

What we will see as we form a consistent practice of praising God is the glorious surprise of the Holy Spirit. This comes about in quite interesting ways. Recently I read about a healing in a book by a healer named Kamila Blessing. She writes of a time when, as a teenager, she was deeply disturbed by the divorce of her parents. As she dealt with this anguish, she had an ongoing difficulty at school. Shy and reserved, she had a math teacher who delighted in tormenting her students. Every morning the teacher would go around the room and ask students if they had done their homework. "Prove it," she would say when a student said they had done the assignment. She would start asking the student questions until they finally broke down. Kamila lived in terror that the teacher would call on her. When she was called upon, she couldn't speak.

Kamila soon became sick and missed twenty-one days of school in a short period of time. "I was alone with the suffering," she writes, "and I didn't know how to pray about it. Soon I became sick about becoming sick."[19]

On the advice of her mother, she decided to start imagining Jesus standing behind her math teacher. This was her way of inviting Jesus into the situation. She was then able to respond easily to the questions, feeling as if she was responding to a warm and loving teacher.

"I could talk when the teacher spoke to me," she writes. "I could find the answer. The Jesus of my imagination always had the consideration to wait while I calmed down and looked for the answer in my mind. He never jumped in and said, 'How come you don't know that?' So I began to look forward to Jesus 'teaching' math. Within two weeks, everything was different. I was healed."[20]

There was an added surprise in this. Blessing writes that soon the teacher became especially kind to her. It was as if they had become special friends. "For the rest of high school," she writes, "that teacher became the first person I would ever have as a genuine colleague."[21]

The surprise in this is that not only had Kamila been healed, but her teacher had been healed as well. She began to exhibit kindness, and this as a result of another person imagining Jesus' presence beside her.

This is just one example of the surprises involved with finding ways to live within the constancy of our God. The fact is that the Holy Spirit cannot be pinned down, but blesses in ways that we cannot anticipate. This surprise does not *require* our leading a life of devotion, for its spontaneity goes even beyond that. But careful attention to God, and finding ways to invite God's presence into our life, does make a difference.

A prayer-centered approach to healing is really a multifaceted experience. At the core is the act of a very simple prayer of faith, one as described by Agnes Sanford. Beyond this is an experience of God on a daily basis. We can open ourselves to this experience through practicing forgiveness and love rather than spite and anger. In performing these actions we truly feed the good branches. God's love becomes more and more apparent upon these branches. That is the heart and soul of prayer-centered healing.

Exercise 5: The Prayer of Faith

Try using the prayer of faith as described by Agnes Sanford. Select some difficulty that you know someone is having, and pray according to the method outlined above. If possible, find others to pray with you. Keep alert for both expected and unexpected results as a result of your prayer.

The Healing Healer

IRENE IS A BEAUTICIAN who has lived her entire life in a small town in North Carolina. Several years ago a great tragedy occurred in her life. Her son, Samuel, was playing at a neighbor's house with some children. One of them took a gun that was leaning against the garage wall and, thinking that it was unloaded, pointed it at Samuel and pulled the trigger. Unfortunately, the gun had a bullet in it, and the boy was killed instantly.

Looking at my own children, I wonder how a parent survives such a tragedy. I saw Irene a number of years after this incident. She was healthy and happy, just as Samuel would have wanted her to be. She had with her a young girl. It turned out that Irene, who is unable to have any more children, looked after this girl quite a bit because of the girl's particular family situation. Irene had become an important part of this young girl's life.

Irene's healing from the emotional damage of a very tragic incident is the result of one important factor discussed in this book. Her life includes a healing act of kindness, a reaching out to someone else in need. Surprisingly, such acts are as healing for the person delivering them as they are for the person in need.

There is in our society something known as the wounded healer. The idea is that those who have been hurt by a particular incident, or suffer from a particular affliction, can benefit by helping others similarly afflicted. Recovering alcoholics help alcoholics, recovering drug addicts help drug addicts, and rape victims volunteer to become rape counselors. The idea behind this is one that speaks both to the helper and the sufferer. The helper is able to heal their wounds while the sufferer receives attention and care from someone who really understands what they are going through. We have already seen the positive benefits of this in Dr. Klitzman's study of HIV-positive individuals. Here volunteerism is one of the ways in which such people can better cope with their condition.

Although the concepts and ideas behind the notion of a wounded healer are solid, I would like to change the term for it to capture better what is really occurring. I would like to refer to the idea of the wounded helping others as the *healing* healer. The reason is this. People who choose to help others, whether they be similarly afflicted or not, are participating in their own healing. They are healing their own physical and psychological wounds. And this is a process that is going to take some time. That is why I don't call it the *healed* healer, because in many instances the healing is going to take a long time, perhaps a lifetime.

Healing in this context refers to the healing of a sufferer who is reaching out to others, trying to participate in their being made whole. They are healing *healers* in that they do try to help others who are afflicted. There are many examples of healing healers. One who was recognized in President Clinton's 1998 State of the Union Address is Suzann Wilson. Suzann's young daughter, Brittany, was one of many children killed at a senseless shooting in a middle school in Jonesboro, Arkansas. This incident received a great deal of attention in the press and on television. Suzann did not withdraw into her grief, although the temptation to do so must have been incredibly strong. She has become a vocal advocate for creating laws that would restrict children's access to guns. In her tragedy there is a healing beauty, and fierceness, as she takes on this noble endeavor. Her words ring strongly as one who has suffered and who is attempting a creative act within her suffering. She does this as a person who was not expecting to be in the limelight. "I'm not very experienced at this," she said in one of her earlier speeches as she stumbled over her prepared speech. Her abilities are growing, however, as she makes efforts to stop senseless violence.

Growing evidence supports the idea that helping others is as good for the helper as for the one being helped. This evidence begins with the fact that good relationships promote health. Dean Ornish's recent *Love and Survival* cites several studies showing just this. Ornish argues, based upon a number of studies, that intimacy and social support are important to health. People who have better relationships with their spouses and families, and who have stronger social and community ties, are at a decreased risk from contracting and dying from such diseases as coronary heart disease, cancer, stroke, respiratory diseases, and other ailments. "In summary," Ornish writes, "love promotes survival."[1]

While acts of altruism are a part of creating strong social ties, they need to be considered in and of themselves. There are studies that do just this. Ornish, for example, cites a 30-year Cornell University study of 427 married women that showed that women who were members of volunteer organizations lived longer. "Specifically," Ornish writes, "52 percent of women who did not belong to a volunteer organization at the beginning of the study were found to have experienced a major illness 30 years later compared with only 36 percent of women who had belonged to a volunteer organization."[2]

Ornish also cites a rather interesting study of students at Harvard University showing that merely watching a documentary movie on altruistic acts can boost the immune system. Students who watched a movie about Mother Teresa's work helping the poor in Calcutta "showed a significant increase in protective antibodies," whereas students who watched a neutral film did not.[3] Ornish concludes from these and other studies that we are "hard-wired to help each other."[4]

Other evidence for the health benefits of altruism may be found in the aptly titled *The Healing Power of Doing Good*. Written by researchers Alan Luks and Peggy Payne, this book is based upon their study of the results of a large-scale survey administered to people who volunteer. The authors found a "healthy helping syndrome" exhibited by people who help others. This included a "helper's high" comparable to a "runners high." Survey respondents said that they enjoyed feelings of warmth and an increase in energy as a result of their efforts. They also described feelings of warmth, euphoria, and a sense of long-lasting calmness.

As far as general health is concerned, helpers identified themselves as healthier than those who do not help. They felt that their improved health began with their volunteerism. They also experienced a good health feeling whenever they remembered acts of helping. Additionally, those who helped once a week identified themselves as healthier than those who did so once a year. Those having personal contact with those they helped had more of the helper's high feeling than did those whose volunteer work did not involve personal contact. Finally, those helping strangers experienced more of the helper's high than did those helping family and friends.[5]

Luks and Payne found that people who help others tend to experience a particularly pleasant feeling that stays with them. They also saw that helpers perceive themselves as being in good physical health. This is by no means an unimportant finding, for studies document that "a person's perceived health status leads to reductions in stress that create actual health improvements."[6]

In short, helping others feels good. This is likely to result in real emotional and physical benefits. I'll use an example of a small event I witnessed recently. Diane is a woman I know who has a teenage daughter attending a local high school. Early in the year a girl from that school committed suicide. This created a great deal of concern both at the school and within the community. School administrators wisely decided that a program should be conducted to help the students deal with their grief and to prevent future suicides. They also decided to conduct a follow-up session a few months later because of the feeling that there may still be underlying anxieties among the students.

A nurse by training, Diane was called in as a medical specialist and as a parent to be part of the program. Diane was a good choice because she was deeply concerned and wanted to help prevent any future actions. When she came back from the event, there was a deep sense of peace about her. She commented that she had "gotten a lot of hugs" from the students. Although her work is often stressful, she maintained a sense of peace throughout the day. She experienced firsthand the benefits of being a *healing* healer.

There is much more that could be written in support of the healing benefits of helping others. For most of us, it just is intuitively true that we feel good when we help. This feeling is the heart and soul of becoming a healing healer. We need to consider in greater detail obstacles to and opportunities for helping. In a world as fast paced and hectic as ours even simple acts of kindness require conscious action.

There are four issues to consider in moving towards becoming a *healing* healer. These are (1) overcoming the "what's in it for me?" syndrome; (2) dealing with responsibilities towards family and friends; (3) avoiding burnout; and (4) finding the time.

The first issue is something that may have occurred to you in reading the above. If helping others leads to a better feeling on the part of the helper, then what would keep someone from engaging in such acts more for their own benefit than for that of the person they are helping. Such an attitude undermines the very meaning of altruism, which implies an unselfish concern for those in need. What if, in helping someone, I am selfishly concerned with my own benefit? Unfortunately, I can see this happening due to the pervasiveness of the "what's in it for me" thinking in our society. Should I be engaging in helpful activities and then run off to have my blood pressure checked to see if this "prescription" works?

Interestingly, the same could be said in relation to the many studies showing the better relative health of those attending church. Would it be wise for me to start attending church just so I can enjoy better health? The comparison of church attendance to altruism is apt here, for it says something about what is really going on. Beyond all of these studies are deeper realities that are harder to quantify. The fact is that altruism, like faith, transforms. It changes us into people experiencing life on the higher branches, to use the metaphor from a previous chapter. It opens us to greater experiences of God's love. This has beneficial physical and psychological health outcomes because it is so consistent with the way we are made by God.

That is why, as Dr. Ornish says, love promotes survival. We are hard-wired to help one another. Acts of kindness are so powerful that in most people just watching a movie of someone doing them has a positive influence. There is something going on here, and that something involves God. It may well be, then, that someone attempting to be a *healing* healer, even though doing it initially for their own good, is likely to be transformed to fit the portrait of a died-in-the wool altruist. They will be acting not for their own good, but for the sake of someone else. The beauty, mystery, and power of this is found in Jesus' words that whomever does acts of kindness for the least among us is thereby doing acts of kindness for him (Mt 25:40).

Another issue with becoming a *healing* healer involves dealing with family responsibilities. More and more people will be called upon in the near future to care for aging grandparents and parents. Yet Luks and Payne found that the healer's high is greater in those helping strangers. It is hard not to think of the parable of the Good Samaritan in thinking about this. This parable is one of the most widely known stories from the Bible. It is frequently preached and probably recognized by most people in our society. The Samaritan in the story is one who stops and helps a beaten and robbed man who is a stranger to him. This is given to us as a model for good behavior.

It is possible to take the information from Luks and Payne, as well as the lesson from the Good Samaritan parable, and apply it to helping a friend or relative. We may feel put upon in helping those we know, forced to do so out of obligation. This often creates resentment.

It is possible, though, to see the stranger in the people we know. By that I mean looking at the ones you are helping as the ones in need. If you find yourself responsible for taking care of relatives, for example, it helps from time to time to see them as one of the many people in this world who are vulnerable. See them not as people you know, but as people whom you have "volunteered" to help. This helps you to refocus, as well as to see your acts as those of beneficence (which they are) rather than those of pure obligation. That is not to say that you should perform them without an eye to your own well-being. In dealing with relatives, just as in dealing with helping people whom one does not know, it is important to avoid burnout.

This brings us to our third issue. Burnout is a common occurrence in our society. It is easy enough to see where it comes from. Many people lead hectic lives. The pace seems much quicker now, in spite of all of the technological innovations that were supposed to save us time and make life easier.

Burnout comes quickly to those helping others. Luks and Payne point out that this was a common complaint among those they surveyed. Respondents at times found that individuals they helped were ungrateful, which wore down the volunteers. Also contributing to burnout was doing work that didn't really fit the interests of the volunteer, as well as helping people who made constant time demands.

Luks and Payne offer several good antidotes to burn-out. Among them are pacing yourself, getting plenty of support, and not trying to rescue the entire world. They also advise to do the kind of helping that comes naturally and to know when to stop.[7] Behind this counsel is the commonsense advice of leading a balanced life. Helping someone is not an excuse to ignore your own needs. Honor your own need to have time to yourself and to do some activities you really enjoy. Set reasonable limits to your helping, but do help. It makes a difference.

A final issue with becoming a *healing* healer is finding the time. For some, this will not be difficult. For many, though, this presents a major obstacle. Those of us with growing children, demanding jobs, interesting hobbies, and various responsibilities know how challenging this can be. Luks and Payne found that the helper's high can result from as little as two hours a week, but just finding those two hours can be difficult.

When finding time is an issue, try to work within your schedule rather than adding to it. For example, I have found some of my most rewarding experiences in helping to coach my children's teams in various sports. Paying attention to my own skills and abilities, I typically am not the head coach, but the assistant coach. This allows me to focus more on the kids, helping them to have a good time rather then on the mechanics of the particular sport, which is not my expertise. I usually spend a little more than two hours a week doing these activities, but since I would be there anyway, either watching the game or the practice from the stands, this really doesn't take time away from my schedule. I get the face-to-face contact that Luks and Payne identify as being part of the helper's high. Since I don't know most of the kids when the season starts, I get the added benefit of helping strangers.

Coaching helps me to be a *healing* healer while I have young children. When my children are older and living away from home, I will have more time to take on other helping activities. In the meantime, I enjoy opportunities to help others within my schedule.

Genuinely helping others, seeing the stranger in those you help, avoiding burnout, and finding time are all important in becoming a *healing* healer. One other element has to do with prayer. Healing efforts should always begin with prayer. Pray for yourself as you initiate and continue healing efforts. Pray that you act with patience and wisdom. Pray for the person you are trying to help, that he or she experience the healing one is looking for or the comfort and support needed. Finally, pray for God's intervention, that God's healing grace be experienced and magnified in all that is done.

Putting this all together, you can ask the following in becoming a *healing* healer:

First, where are you in need of healing? I was once asked to write a spiritual autobiography as part of a program in spiritual direction. I was specifically asked to write about where I felt closest to God and where "life hurts." You might take on this last part of the task in finding where you need healing. You probably know of the obvious hurts, but perhaps there are some not so obvious ones as well. This is useful information in becoming a *healing* healer, for we know that those working with the similarly afflicted tend to find healing within their own lives. Answering this question may be important in understanding where you can help others.

Second, what enlivens you? There is nothing worse then taking on an extra task that you find boring and tedious. You probably won't stay at it long. Instead, look at your interests and abilities. Additionally, look for something that gives you some kind of spark. If you really like being around young people, then that is a place to look. If the thought of working with someone from another culture is exciting, then that presents some possibilities.

Third, what are the needs in the people around you? This question might supersede the answers to the above questions. You might be presented with an obligation to help a friend or a relative. This presents a different set of needs. However, going through all of these questions can be helpful. You might ask, for example, how to relate your needs to those of the person you are helping. You might also look for things that are consistent with your interests. If you like to go to movies, for example, then you might be able to take the person you care for to the movies on a regular basis.

Fourth, if there isn't anyone in your life you currently have responsibility for, then you can look more intently at your community. What are the needs there? How can you match those to your particular need for healing or to your interests?

Fifth, what does your schedule allow? Be reasonable as you look at your schedule. How much time do you have to dedicate to helping others? Look for places where you can work within your schedule. You may be running into people in need all of the time as part of your daily routine and just not thinking about it. Take the time to consider how you can help.

Sixth, how can you stay positive? Realize that helping is not always going to be fun. You are not always going to get the helper's high. Like running or other types of exercise, there will be times when you simply don't want to do it. Yet, again like running, there will be times after you put in that first bit of effort that the good feeling returns. Be realistic about this, and stay focused upon your attitude as well. Identify the ways you need to look at the world that will help you maintain your healing efforts.

Answering the above questions will help you to identify how you, as an individual, can become a healing healer. They also help you to understand what will keep you motivated to continue your healing efforts. Two other recommendations I make are to maintain a sense of prayer in all of your healing efforts, and to be open to the healing that will take place in your life and the lives of the people around you. In this chapter we have not discussed the miraculous side of healing. That is because the focus here is a more practical one. The theme has been that helping others feels good and has a healing quality about it, both for you and for the person you help. Staying focused on prayer as you undertake your healing efforts adds another dimension to an already deep experience. Recognize that your *helping* efforts towards others are *healing* efforts, healing yourself, the person you help, and the world. Undertake them prayerfully.

Let's conclude with a story that illustrates much of the above, as well as something of how God's miracles take place in often unsuspected and unplanned ways. A friend of mine is a priest who often volunteers to go to Haiti to care for people who live in very impoverished conditions. He tells the true story of a doctor who went there as part of a medical mission. The doctor saw many conditions, some of which he could treat, others he could not.

One day a young boy came to the clinic with his grandfather, a man who had been blind from birth. The old man was not only blind but also in a rather disheveled and unkempt condition. Scorned by the community, he lived in a hut at the outside of the village, isolated and alone except for his grandson.

The boy asked if there was not something that could be done for the man. The doctor looked at the man and knew immediately that there was nothing that could be done. The man had been born without eyes. There was nothing in his training that could help this. He told the boy that there was nothing he could do. Wanting to do something, however, he called a priest over and together with some others that were present they laid hands on this man and prayed for his healing.

A few years later the doctor returned to the same area of Haiti as part of another healing mission. Although the boy was a little older, he recognized the doctor immediately when he came to visit. The doctor's lack of ability to help the boy's grandfather had weighed on his mind. The boy, however, was grateful, jubilant in fact.

"You can't believe how you have helped my grandfather," the boy said.

"You mean the blind man?" the doctor said with disbelief.

"Yes."

The doctor inquired further from the boy and others and found out the following. After the man's blindness was prayed for something indeed miraculous had taken place. The man experienced a gradual transformation back in his community. He felt better and dressed better. More importantly, he became a man of insight. People began coming to him with their problems, for he had great wisdom and was able to help them through their difficulties. No longer shunned and at the edges of the community, he was at the very center, a great and wise leader who gave insightful advice. The man himself had become a *healing* healer.

Here we see an example of God's ways. God did heal this man from blindness, but granted him vision in a different way. He gave him the ability to "see" into people's problems, and to help them find ways of coping with them.

It is this kind of experience that I would like you to be open to as you begin your healing efforts. God does indeed work in mysterious ways. They are also the ways of healing. A *healing* healer is granted the opportunity of participating in this process.

Exercise Six: Where Are You Called?

"The place God calls you is to the place where your deep gladness and the world's deep hunger meet."[8] This statement from writer Frederick Buechner is one of the best I've seen in helping people to discover where God might be calling them to heal. Spend twenty to thirty minutes pondering this statement. Write down your thoughts as you do so. Conclude by writing a few paragraphs, explaining where your deep gladness and the world's deep hunger meet. Finally, do something within the next week that fits with what you have written.

Healing Notions

"IT IS MORE BLESSED TO GIVE than to receive." I have heard this expression a number of times in my life. I had a hard time understanding it when I was younger. I often thought of it just after Christmas as I enjoyed all of the gifts I received. How could it be better to give when receiving was such a thrill?

As I grew I realized the truth of the expression. There is a special feeling involved in giving to others. It far exceeds my experience in receiving, for at some level receiving never really satisfies, while giving reaches some deeper part of the soul.

Still, the experience of giving is not well captured by the statement, "It is more blessed to give than to receive." These words fail to express what is taking place. They separate notions that are really connected. It is better to say that in giving we receive. This is precisely what the Peace Prayer of Saint Francis says. "In giving we receive," the prayer says, just as in pardoning "we are pardoned." In acting for the benefit of others, as well as in forgiving others, we act upon our connection to them. We understand that this expression of love, in some form or fashion, is reflected back to us in the form of a blessing. Giving puts us upon the branches of the more joyous universe.

This is precisely why I feel more connected and whole when I pray for the healing of others. Such prayers take me much deeper. They are prayers in which I am able to move past my own concerns.

The interplay between giving and receiving is the first of some remaining elements we consider as we reach towards our conclusions concerning faith and healing. In this chapter we examine further notions involved in creating a life of healing. After each of these elements, I offer personal observations concerning the joys and difficulties involved in applying these notions to life.

The notion that in giving we receive is the logical outcome of many of the ideas we have explored thus far. Healing involves actions such as a concern for others, forgiveness, and a surrendering to God. Each of these in turn requires a dying to the self so that we experience the true joy of giving to others. This brings us to a statement of our first notion in constructing a life of healing:

- In healing we must understand that we are connecting with the truth that "in giving we receive."

In my job as a manager I often have to struggle with my tendency not to listen to the opinions of others. This is painful to admit since I have always prided myself on considering the thoughts of others. Still, instances occur when the work becomes hectic and someone makes a demand that I feel I really can't do anything about. Rather than listen to what the person is saying, I verbally list the reasons why what they ask simply can't be done. Naturally, if someone is in emotional or physical difficulty and making a request that I feel I can't do anything about, there isn't much room for healing with such an attitude. In order to apply the element above, I must learn to slow down and find out what I can give so that both of us can better our chances of receiving a blessing.

Another notion in creating a life of healing is the willingness to try to heal. By that I mean a willingness actually to pray for a healing in expectation that something will take place. This idea is found within the writings of Agnes Sanford. In *The Healing Light*, Sanford encourages readers to undertake experiments in healing. "One way to understand a hitherto unexplored force of nature," she writes, "is to experiment with that force intelligently and with an open mind."[1] She encourages readers to select something to pray for, and to keep praying for it.

I initially had reservations about taking this approach. It seems that it might easily fall into the errors of (1) expecting God to prove God's existence—that is, asking for a sign; (2) putting myself and my needs at the center instead of God—that is, asking what God can do for me instead of what I can do for God; and (3) creating a situation where I might begin to question my own faith—that is, questioning God's power when God doesn't "come through" with a healing.

These are serious concerns. We must remember, though, that asking God to do something is not beyond the pale of Scripture. Jesus says, "Very truly, I tell you, if you ask anything of the Father in my name, he will give it to you. Until now you have not asked for anything in my name. Ask and you will receive, so that your joy may be complete" (Jn 16:23–24).

Luke contains language equally as strong. Here Jesus says:

> So I say to you, Ask, and it will be given you; search, and you will find; knock, and the door will be opened for you. For everyone who asks receives, and everyone who searches finds, and for everyone who knocks, the door will be opened. Is there anyone among you who, if your child asks for a fish, will give a snake instead of a fish? Or if the child asks for an egg, will give a scorpion? If you then, who are evil, know how to give good gifts to your children, how much more will the heavenly Father give the Holy Spirit to those who ask him! (Lk 11:9–13).

The idea of asking a parent for something is a useful model to help us to overcome the three concerns stated above. In a healthy parent-child relationship, we would not ask a parent for something so that they might "prove" that they are our parents or that they love us. We ask that they do something out of their love for us. That is effective in helping us to understand what to approach God about in prayer. Just as I would be concerned about a request from my own children for a faster and newer sports car, God might look at our own requests as indicative of an undeveloped spiritual life. Asking to receive relief from a physical ailment, however, is a different matter. This sentiment matches James' statement that, "You do not have, because you do not ask. You ask and do not receive, because you ask wrongly, in order to spend what you get on your pleasures" (Jas 4:2–3).

The parent-child approach also addresses the second and third concerns. Asking for something to happen does not necessarily mean that I am placing myself at the center. Now this might be the case if all I ask for are material things. But asking for something to happen out of a sense of compassion is certainly not outside of the realm of what a child could rightly ask a parent. Finally, if the healing sought does not take place, this need not cause me to question the power or authority of "God the parent." It is simply that "God knows best." Although this is a particularly difficult pill to swallow in an age where all authority tends to be questioned, it is simply the fact that God knows more (indeed, all) about the universe. A request, even for my own healing, may not be for the good of the universe. At some point, we have to trust God to know best.

All this is to say that it is acceptable to ask for healing as Sanford recommends. A careful reading of the passage from Luke indicates that we should do precisely that. Ask. This leads us to our next statement:

- Ask, and expect a blessing.

I have had a difficult time overcoming my reluctance to ask. When I consider my own petty ailments, they hardly seem worth troubling God over. I overcame this, though, by realizing that I was somewhat reluctant to pray about anything in my life for the same reason. I just didn't think that things were important enough to bother God.

I slowly realized that in occasionally asking for some small healing that I became experienced in praying for larger ones. In fact, I have had success in praying for the smaller things. This has bolstered my confidence in both asking and receiving. This has also tended to focus my prayers. In the past my prayers wandered. Now I am much clearer in my prayers, unafraid both to ask for a blessing while at the same time asking how I can be a blessing to others.

Another healing notion has to do with contact. I mean this in two ways. There is the contact of being in a community where we share with others our concerns and our praises. Another way is that of physical contact or touch.

We have already seen the importance of community in our discussions of the work of Dean Ornish and others. People who have more connections within their community, who volunteer and who attend worship services, tend to be in better health. The importance of community is also found within the Scriptures. The Bible says, "Where two or three are gathered in my name, I am there among them" (Mt 18:20). The implication of this statement is that being with others is important to God. It is not always the case that group prayer is better than individual prayer, but certainly people gathering together to pray for healing are finding remarkable consequences as a result of their efforts. I believe that healing prayer groups are where the Spirit is leading us today.

Contact in the sense of touch is also important. We know that Jesus often touched, or was touched by, those whom he healed. The laying on of hands continues as an integral part of the Church's tradition. Francis MacNutt's *Healing* discusses the importance of touch in modern instances of healing. MacNutt describes a "warm current of healing power" that often flows from the healer to the sick person.[2] The feeling of an electric current in the hands of the healer is a common experience in accounts of healing.

Another aspect of healing touch is that it often leads to a deep experience of love on the part of the person who is sick. "After a group has gathered round and prayed for a person," MacNutt writes, "that person is usually sorry to see the prayer end. There is a sense of community and love experienced in a very deep way."[3] Countless studies show the importance of touch to the experience of well-being. We take this for granted when it comes to infants and children. It is also true, however, that there is something very healing about touch in adults as well. In fact, there is even a school of therapeutic touch that has some popularity within the medical community.

Of course, the whole notion of touch is somewhat problematic in our society. Unlike many other cultures, people in the United States tend not to touch a great deal. Additionally, the fear of sexual harassment (which is not an ungrounded fear since it does happen) has even further limited our willingness to touch.

I recall, however, an instance when I attended a small meeting of people who were interested in healing. I was introduced to one woman, a healer, who looked to be in her mid fifties. I extended my hand to greet her and she said, "In my church we don't shake hands, we hug." She proceeded to give me a hug. I immediately experienced a deep sense of warmth and love.

All of this is to say that in our society we must still chose our moments of contact very carefully. There is nothing worse than unwelcome physical contact. At the same time, look for and enjoy opportunities where healing contact, whether it be a laying on of hands or a simple hug, can take place.

The importance of both communal and physical contact brings us to the following statement:

- To heal and be healed, seek a healing community where appropriate physical contact is encouraged.

I have to admit that this remains one of the more problematic areas for me. As an introvert, I do not naturally gravitate towards meetings and groups. I often feel awkward in approaching such groups, and often feel a need to recharge my batteries afterwards. Additionally, I, too, am a creature of our society, and am not always comfortable with laying on of hands and hugs. I am reminded of a quote that is supposedly from the famous Harvard philosopher and psychologist from the early part of this century, William James. "People in our society would rather attend a lecture about heaven than actually to go there." It is one thing to have an intellectual understanding of the importance of community relations and physical contact. It is quite another to put these into practice.

Bowing to my own nature, I have learned to pick and chose the meetings I go to. I realize that attending a lot of them would simply leave me exhausted. I have also undertaken a practice of easing into groups involved with healing so that I get a comfort level with what is occurring. I am doing the same with the physical side of healing.

Another notion in healing is to attempt to understand why healing may not take place. We have alluded to possible reasons for such an occurrence, but it is worth mentioning again because this is such a troubling issue for so many. The best explanation of why healing may not take place is found in MacNutt's work. In *Healing* he enumerates twelve reasons why, in his experience, healing may not take place. These are

1. Lack of faith
2. Redemptive suffering
3. A false value attached to suffering
4. Sin
5. Not praying specifically (or for the root cause of suffering)
6. Faulty diagnosis
7. Refusal to see God's medicine as a way God heals

8. Not using the natural means of preserving health
9. "Now is not the time..."
10. A different person is to be the instrument of healing
11. Demonic influence
12. The social environment prevents healing from taking place[4]

These reasons well capture the physical, emotional, and spiritual issues that may be involved in someone not being healed. Here we see that the right illness may not have been identified, the root cause may not be being prayed for, or the right person may not be involved in the healing. Additionally, there may be outside forces with which to contend, or it may be suffering that an individual must go through for some reason. Also, it may be that either the sick person or the environment in which they live needs to change. Finally, it just might not be time.

One healer offered me a much shorter explanation for why healing may not take place. "I can almost tell whether or not a person will be healed," he said. "It's those who refuse to make the necessary changes in their lives who will not be healed." An inner willingness to change, coupled with a strong desire to pray frequently and have others pray for them, contributes to the likelihood that prayer will have a positive result.

This brings us to the following element in prayer:

- Pray hard and with awareness, noting the changes that you, with the help of the Holy Spirit, must undertake.

Like many people in today's society, one of my chief "conditions" is job-related stress. This is not something I take lightly, for this was a contributing factor to my father's death from a heart attack. I have even gone so far as to pray for the reduction of stress in my life. Still, it remains a chronic condition.

In dealing with this issue, I remain impressed with the need for personal change. If I want to reduce my feeling of stress, then I must do more than pray. I must also look at my reactions to life, as well as my habits, and make changes to reduce the amount of stress.

The antidote to stress is found within David Steindl-Rast's *Gratefulness, the Heart of Prayer*. My attitude has become one of creating a void within myself so that I can experience more of the fullness of God. This void allows me to lessen the grip of whatever is causing me stress. This is captured by Steindl-Rast's "definition" of zero. This is a concept he introduces late in his book to express the need to empty ourselves so that we have room for Christ. He says of zero that it's very shape, "written as 0, expresses emptiness. But the full circle also signifies fullness. Zero stands for nothing, but by adding zero to a number we can multiply it tenfold, a hundredfold, a thousandfold. Gratefulness gives fullness to life by adding nothing. Understanding 0 by becoming 0—that's what gratefulness is all about."[5]

This is good advice for me, for it reminds me that too much concern with myself, which is often the root of my stress, is toxic. It also leaves little room for the healing presence of Christ. Letting go of myself is the change I must undertake in order to experience a healing from stress. It creates a void that only God can fill, which in turn leads to healing gratefulness on my part.

The last element in creating a life of healing is the importance of establishing a pattern of connecting with God. Many turn to prayer when something goes awry. Although this is certainly understandable, imagine the comfort and strength involved with having a daily practice of prayer. In fact, data is mounting to support the health benefits of a personal as well as a communal practice of faith.

Benedictine spirituality provides helpful examples here. Best selling books by Kathleen Norris and Joan Chittister attest to the growing popularity of this approach to life. Benedictine spirituality derives from the practices of Benedictine monastics. Although it may seem that monks and nuns have nothing to say to those of us living in the world, in fact some of the notions supporting this life have quite a rich application to our own.

Contemporary writers are making a connection between Benedictine practices and healing. Writer Esther de Waal, for example, describes the Rule of Saint Benedict, upon which the Benedictine life is based, as a "handbook of healing."[6] Writers such as Frank Bianco and Kathleen Norris also emphasize the importance of healing and monasticism. Bianco's moving book, *Voices of Silence: Lives of the Trappists Today*, recounts many true stories of the healing influence of monasticism upon those living under the Cistercian (or strict observance) form of Benedictine monasticism. He also tells of his own healing from the emotional wounds left by the untimely death of his son, Michael.[7] *The Cloister Walk* is Kathleen Norris' account of the influence of Benedictine practices and spirituality upon her life. It, too, is filled with both subtle and pronounced tales of emotional healing.[8]

When we get down to the heart of the matter, the healing pattern established by Benedictine spirituality is that of presence, practice, and simplicity. The Benedictine monastic is to keep God at the center, experiencing God's presence in all that they do. The focus is on encountering God not in the reverie of a religious experience, but in the ordinary things of life. As de Waal puts it, "The Rule does not call us to heroic deeds. Instead Saint Benedict is telling me that my way to God lies in the daily and the ordinary. If I cannot find God here and now, in my home and in my work, in my daily routine, in the things that I handle in the kitchen or in the office, then it is no good looking for him anywhere else."[9]

Among the ways of encountering God are through practice. The monastic life is a life of prayerful practices. Daily reading of the Scriptures, and meditating upon their content, are key ingredients to the life as laid out in Saint Benedict's Rule. Important, too, is the practice of carrying the results of biblical-based contemplation into the daily walk of life. "The Lord waits for us daily," writes Saint Benedict, "to translate into action, as we should, his holy teachings."[10]

Simplicity is a trait that runs throughout the Rule, just as it does throughout the practice of monastics. At the center of the three vows that Benedictines take—stability, conversion, and obedience—is a life built upon simple spiritual practices and humility. This is a life void of the striving for more income and greater social prestige.

Presence, practice, and simplicity all contribute to the healing of many of the maladies associated with modern life. While we will talk further about spiritual practice in the next chapter, we will start here with the advice of how to incorporate a spiritual practice into your life. Data is accumulating to show that personal spiritual practices are correlated with better health practices. Researcher Harold Koenig, M.D., for example, finds that there is less alcohol and nicotine addiction among those who engage in such personal spiritual practice as daily Bible reading.[11] Koenig's book, *The Healing Power of Faith*, also provides numerous case studies in which an individual's decision to engage in a daily spiritual practice either contributed to healing or to a better coping with a particular condition.

This brings us to our final element of healing:

- Practice such simple daily spiritual exercises as Bible study combined with prayer.

I have tried a number of spiritual exercises over the years. I have tried centering prayer, contemplation, and time for praise, to name just a few. All of these have merit. What I keep returning to, however, is scriptural study. Indeed, the above practices are well augmented by beginning with a reading of the Bible.

One of the most difficult parts of any practice is maintaining the discipline to do it. I find that it is best to have a spiritual practice at the beginning, in the middle, and at the end of the day. There is a big difference in my energy level and in the way I approach the situations I face when I do this. Each time, however, has its obstructions. To read and pray early in the morning involves getting up at a certain time. To do the same in the middle of the day involves refraining for a few minutes from checking my messages while I was away at lunch. To pursue a practice at the end of the day means not getting in a hurry to eat or to tackle whatever project may be awaiting me at home.

Simple spiritual practices involve simple spiritual disciplines. It means getting up at the right time, pausing in the middle of the day, and slowing down at the end of the day. While these disciplines may at times prove difficult, they are well worth the effort.

Finding a life of spiritual-based healing involves, as we have seen, the following:

1. In healing we must understand that we are connecting with the truth that "in giving we receive."
2. Ask, and expect a blessing.
3. To heal and be healed, seek a healing community where appropriate physical contact is encouraged.
4. Pray hard and with awareness, noting the changes that you, with the help of the Holy Spirit, must undertake.
5. Practice such simple daily spiritual exercises as Bible study combined with prayer.

These five healing notions are ways to open the door to God's healing love. They allow us to experience the real connection between giving and receiving.

Exercise 7: Reflective Healing

Take a moment to reflect upon the kind of day you had today. If you are reading this in the morning, think about the kind of day you had yesterday. What simple practices could you have put in place to make it a better one? Could you have spent a few moments reading the Bible in the morning? Would things have been better if you had taken a moment to go talk to someone whom you hadn't talked to in a while? Identify at least one thing and put it into practice in the coming days.

Simple Methods

I REMEMBER STANDING in rapture in front of a Vincent Van Gogh painting at the Van Gogh Museum in Amsterdam. *Is something like this ever going to come along again?* I thought. A friend of mine, Rev. Carter Paden, had much the same thought when viewing a Michelangelo statue in Rome. He expressed his feeling more in theological terms. *When*, he asked himself, *has the Holy Spirit expressed itself in just this way, with just this beauty and power?*

Art is often like that. Something very unique is expressed, a work of power and deep meaning, but also something which could not have been predicted.

The work of the Holy Spirit in healing has that element about it. That is why healing is hard to predict. It happens at unexpected times and in unanticipated ways. Francis MacNutt gives us two illustrations of this. One is of a famous healer, Kathryn Kuhlman, who was often asked to write a book about how and why healing took place. When she thought she had it all figured out, however, some healing would take place that would not fit with what she was about to write. She found it impossible to capture what was going on because the Holy Spirit had a way of doing something contrary to what she had said.[1]

Another illustration concerns an avowed skeptic of healing. MacNutt writes of a priest who conducted a healing service at a conference with the intent of teaching people that such things don't work and to be wary of them. At one point during the service he called up to the altar anyone who wanted to be healed. Several came up and the priest laid his hands upon them. To his amazement, some of the people who came forward were genuinely healed.[2]

Although the Spirit may be unpredictable, certain things do correlate with health and healing, just as they do with the creation of a masterpiece. Artists are people who are born with certain talents and who discipline themselves so that those talents may be expressed. Similarly, certain beliefs and practices can be cultivated in order to increase the possibility of health and healing.

We begin this chapter by outlining a simple method. It is simple in that it consists of five easily followed steps. These steps are based upon the research I have conducted into factors that increase healing and health. It is important that you tailor the steps of this method to fit your life, filling out the method in a way that will work for you. "Pray as you can, not as you can't" is an expression I have come across lately. For most of us, adopting practices that are difficult or feel uncomfortable is simply too hard to do. That is why I offer the steps as an invitation for you to create a life of healing. These steps will help you to create daily practices consistent with health and healing. At the end of each of the steps is an italicized section asking you to do something to apply the step to your life. We conclude this chapter by describing a healing service that is also very simple, though nonetheless effective and deeply moving.

Step One: Acknowledging God

It is no mistake that twelve-step programs begin by acknowledging a higher Power. Acknowledging God takes the pressure off of our own feeble attempts to control our desires and our environment. "Blessed are the poor in spirit," Jesus says in the beatitudes. One interpretation of this is that those who recognize their own weakness, and thus see their need to lean upon God, are indeed blessed. This is the beginning of a faith-based approach to healing.

Debbie was a graduate of a prestigious university who always prided herself on her intellectual ability. She had managed to become fairly successful in business, although aspects of her personality kept her from moving up as high in the corporate ladder as she would have liked. Her life started to unravel just as she turned forty. Her position was eliminated as part of an effort to get rid of mid-level management. She was forced to take a lower-level position with a competitor. Although this new job had a lot of promise, Debbie could not get over her anger at having lost her old one. Always a drinker, she started to drink even more. She even began having a few drinks during lunch, believing that even impaired she could still outthink her bosses and coworkers.

Debbie was convinced that her noon drinking went unnoticed. She was totally surprised when one day she was confronted about her drinking and fired on the spot. This led to nearly a year of continued drinking and denial in which Debbie ended up separated from her husband and children and living in a small downtown apartment. Then one day she started thinking about God. She had always held an intellectual contempt about any belief in a deity. She refused to believe in God unless God's existence could be proven. When she was a student she had researched all of the proofs of God's existence she could find. All of them, in her opinion, came up short. She remained a committed agnostic.

She sat on the couch of the apartment where she was living, contemplating her condition and even thinking about taking her own life. At one point she glanced out the window, looking at the cross on a steeple that was barely visible above the buildings. She knew it was time to make a decision. The way she looked at life just didn't work. While her reason told her that God's existence could not be indisputably proven, her heart told her that something was there if only she chose to believe. She finally got down on her knees and prayed. Then she walked to the church whose steeple had been beckoning to her ever since she moved into the apartment. There she found a

pastor who listened. Debbie was soon an active member
of that church and in the Alcoholics Anonymous group
that met there. While she has had a couple of setbacks,
she has now been sober for a long, long time. While much
has helped her on her way, the turning point in her life
was the simple acknowledgment of God.

*The first step of the twelve-step program for alcohol-
ics and other addicted people is to acknowledge the existence of a higher Power, whatever you conceive that
power to be. Acknowledge God and then take a few
moments to write down what you conceive God to be.
This is an important exercise because though we may do
a lot of talking about God, we often don't think enough
about what God is. Although God does "surpass all understanding" there are still attributes of God's existence
that we experience. After you have done this, focus specifically on God the healer. What is your understanding
of God in this important aspect? Finally, take time to
acknowledge and praise God in all God's glory. Acknowledge and praise God for a few minutes each day.*

Step Two: Prayer Time

Prayer makes a difference. We saw in the last chapter that people who have a private devotional
practice, in addition to attending public worship
service, tend to be healthier both psychologically
and emotionally. Connecting with God regularly
is essential for the Christian. It is one of the building blocks of our lives.

Richard Mullis is a friend of mine who relatively late in life took up the practice of a regular routine of prayer. He added a noonday practice in addition to his morning and evening prayers. He felt a deep sense of peace and wholeness as a result of what may seem to be a small thing. He hardly thought about this being externally visible to others. On a yearly visit to see a married couple named Bob and Linda who live several hundred miles away, Richard had an interesting experience.

"You seem more at peace with yourself, Richard," Bob said, noting that Richard no longer appeared as stressed and cynical as he used to be.

"When did you become so religious?" Linda said in a separate conversation.

Both comments surprised Richard since he had not discussed with them any religious topics. Nor had he talked about his private devotionals. He had been healed from a negative and abrasive attitude, which was in turn recognized by his friends.

There is a very real sense in which Christ finds a way to enter our lives through prayer. Begin a practice of prayerfully turning to God at the beginning, in the middle, and at the end of the day. Use one of these times for prayerful scriptural reading, one for silent meditation, and one for praying the prayer of faith. For this last prayer, pick a condition that either you or someone else has that you would like to see healed. Set aside twenty minutes each week to record any feelings you have or events that occur in a faith journal.

Step Three: Gentle Reminders

> An old idea that is making a comeback is that of practicing the presence of God. This means remembering to experience God in the daily moments of your life. One means of doing this is by recalling a phrase throughout the day that brings you closer to God. Such phrases may come from anywhere. They may derive from personal Scripture reading or from a worship service. Look for words that speak to you and that remind you of God's presence, and then repeat them throughout the day. You'll want to keep the words for some length of time, though you don't need to feel as if you must keep them forever. The words you choose will change as you change.

I have used this method recently to deal with my tendency to worry over events that I encounter in life. I have been reading Jan Karon's wonderful books about the fictitious town of Mitford, North Carolina. Karon's main characters are an Episcopal priest named Tim Kavanaugh and his wife, Cynthia. The Kavanaugh's often turn their concerns over to God. At times when they are most troubled or when they face something that is totally out of control, they remember to pray the "prayer that never fails." While this is not revealed at first, it finally becomes clear what this prayer is. It is, "Thy will be done." This prayer is a wonderful way of dealing with the difficult circumstances of life, for it allows us at last to turn our concerns over to our Maker. It is also a phrase I have used frequently throughout the course of the day to deal with stress. It reminds me who is really in control.

These words helped me recently as I went through the process of hiring a new employee. I always go through such a process with trepidation. Having worked in Human Resources, I know of all the mistakes that supervisors and managers can make in hiring. I have also had the experience of finding a person who I thought was just right for the job, only to have him or her turn me down for one reason or another. Finally, not being one to take rejection well, I always hate to be the one who is doing the rejecting.

As I went through this latest round, however, I recalled the prayer that never fails. This served as a gentle reminder, allowing me to calm down and maintain a sense of perspective. Such a practice may not guarantee the "best" outcome for you as an individual, but remember that it is not your will that is manifested. "Thy will be done" is an excellent prayer for keeping sanity in a world where we simply don't call all of the shots.

Write down a word or phrase now that reminds you of God's close presence to you. Use this as a gentle reminder throughout the day. At the end of the day think back upon your experience as you recited the words. How were the words healing ones for you? How did they help you to deal with any affliction you may have?

Step Four: Helping Others

> Altruism is a powerful means of creating health
> and wellness. It really is true that in helping oth-
> ers we help ourselves. Yet in a time when sched-
> ules are tight and demands on our time many, it
> is hard to find the space in our lives for this. Luck-
> ily, altruism appears to be very similar to exercise
> in that even a small amount goes a long way.

While acknowledging God, prayer and gentle remind-
ers are helpful to health and healing, it is important to
have an active component to your healing. As we have
seen, there is nothing like face-to-face contact with others who are in need. This puts our faith into practice, and
makes a world of difference in the way we feel about life.

There are many, many ways you can help others. It
may be through doing something you simple enjoy doing, or it may be through putting some particular skill
you have developed to use in a volunteer setting. I know
people who participate in programs teaching literacy to
adults, for example, not because they have any special
skill at it, but because they enjoy it. On the other hand, I
know a lawyer who took up a Lenten practice of providing free legal advice to the poor, using her formal training as a way to help those in need.

Of course, if you are suffering from a particular ailment, it is also helpful to help those who are similarly
afflicted. You are uniquely qualified to help people who
are similar to you.

Whatever your affliction or your time constraints, there is something you can do to help others. Take time each week to identify something you can do. It need not be something you feel is earthshaking. Begin by picking something simple, and then expand it as your time allows. Do this without the expectation that you will get something in return, but purely for the joy of helping others. Do it in the spirit of altruism.

Step Five: Find a Healing Community

A final step in healing and health is finding a community. We have seen from Dr. Ornish and others that belonging in a community is extremely important to maintaining health. Studies show that those who are involved in their community and who have strong social ties are healthier.

There are ways of finding community. One is by attending some kind of worship service. Time and again studies show that people who attend worship services are healthier and happier than those who do not. The divorce rates are lower, the alcoholism rate is lower, and the incidence of depression is lower. The simple act of going to church is a monumental first step in finding a community.

Another way of finding a community specifically related to healing is to join a healing group or participate in a healing service. Many churches are now conducting healing services, and this is a good place of finding a community and participating in a healing service at the same time. There are also churches that sponsor a variety of groups that meet for the purpose of healing. I have found, in fact, a whole network of healing groups in my small community. All you have to do is start looking, and you are bound to find something you like.

Ask your priest or minister about healing. If they themselves do not belong to or participate in a healing service, they are bound to know someone who does. Begin a list of healing contacts. Keep adding to the list until you feel comfortable that you have found the healing community that is right for you. Look for a place where you feel uniquely at home. This is one where you feel loved and supported so that you are free to share your concerns and to ask for healing.

Hopefully, you can use the steps above to create a life of healing. This is a life where you learn to rely upon God and where you also find others to help you in your journey to healing. One aspect of healing you may be particularly interested in is the healing service. Many may feel reluctant to participate in such a service. At the same time, there is much to be gained from searching for healing in just this way.

In this regard, I will now describe a healing service that I feel is particularly effective. Signal Mountain Presbyterian is a large church located on a ridge high above the city of Chattanooga. The church began a healing service nearly four years ago at the request of both members and elders. Although I am not Presbyterian, I had heard good things about this service. I also knew that King Oehmig, whom I have mentioned earlier in this book, had a hand in designing the service.

Before attending I called the pastor, Dr. William Dudley, to discuss what is involved in the service. I found him warm and personable and very willing to talk at length about the service. He explained that the service is held on the third Sunday of each month at 5:30 P.M. The third Sunday was selected to be symbolic of the Trinity. Rev. Dudley explained that nearly half of the people who attend this service are not Presbyterians, and that it is truly an ecumenical service.

I felt apprehensive as I drove up the mountain Sunday afternoon. Even though the service had been explained to me, I was still concerned that this would be an uncomfortable experience. Would I feel out of place because I didn't have any major physical problem? Would I find the service too emotional or inauthentic?

I parked my car in the church lot and prayed silently for a few minutes. Then I left my car and walked through the church doors to a large sanctuary where the service was to be conducted. The sanctuary appeared empty, but I was then directed to an area tucked away to the side of the altar. From there I could see the entire sanctuary.

People slowly trickled in, some embracing, some just quietly slipping into one of the pews. There were around forty people assembled by the time the ministers entered at 5:30. I was impressed once more by Rev. Dudley's warmth and genuineness as he began speaking to the crowd. He explained the mechanics of the service, taking care to address questions newcomers might have. He pointed out that this was a service of healing and thanksgiving, noting that we should give thanks to God for what occurs. He told of a reconciliation that had taken place between two people as a result of a recent healing service. He also nodded to one person, a hairless but smiling young woman, who had recently received a clean lab report.

Rev. Dudley remembered that last time they had held the service in a smaller room of the church. The particular Scripture they had studied on that occasion was that of the young paralytic whose friends had lowered him through the roof to be before Jesus. The minister explained that the feel of the last service contributed to a direct understanding of that passage. The room was crowded and people had to step over one another to participate in the service. This was similar to what the crowd in the Scripture passage must have experienced.

This time the setting was equally apt. The Scripture to be studied today was that of the woman who had been suffering from bleeding for twelve years, and who touched Jesus' robe from the back in order to be healed. Rev. Dudley pointed out that this woman would probably have had to make her way through a large crowd to get close to Jesus.

"Imagine," Rev. Dudley said, pointing to the wall on the far side of the sanctuary, "traveling through a crowd that reached back to there."

After Rev. Dudley's brief introduction the service began with some simple songs of praise. These were simple

songs that set the mood for the rest of the service. Next
Rev. Dudley got back up and read the Scripture related
to the woman who had suffered from an affliction for
twelve years. He pointed out the persistence she must
have had, for even with a longstanding health problem
she was still willing to seek healing. He said that many,
including himself, are often reluctant to ask God for healing because we feel that we are too trivial to concern
God with our problems. Surely God, who is so great and
powerful, does not have time for people as small and
unworthy as are we.

Yet we are encouraged to ask for healing. Rev. Dudley
praised the woman who had touched Jesus' robe for her
courage and her belief. Likewise he wanted us to realize
that we are each important in God's eyes, and should not be
afraid to lay our concerns and burdens before our Savior.

After the Scripture reading and the brief comments
there was a eucharistic celebration, followed by the actual time for healing. Rev. Dudley sat down in the front
pew with the elders. They would sit with their backs to
those assembled, he had explained earlier, so that no one
would feel pressured to come forward. Those who wanted
to come forward and be prayed for could do so, while
others could pray quietly by themselves or with prayer
partners in the pews. Those who did come forward were
encouraged to go either to himself or to one of the elders.

A small number of people came forward to be with
the minister and elders. When they did so, they explained
their afflictions privately to those who would pray over
them. The elders or the minister then asked if they wanted

to be anointed with oil. Next they asked if it was accept-able for them to touch the person while they prayed. Following this, the healers positioned themselves around the person, laid hands upon him or her, and began praying. The prayer involved petitioning for the affliction to be healed, as well as asking that the person be given the strength to change whatever may be needed in his or her life in order to receive healing. The final part of the prayer was a demand that if any demons or spirits were involved that they be cast out. After the prayer the healers sat with the person for as long as was needed, offering talk and reassurance.

I experienced a deep sense of peace watching this service. The Holy Spirit was present here. I could see it in the faces of those who stepped forward to be healed as well as in those praying for them. Moreover, I could feel it in my bones.

This type of service has much to offer, and may be adapted and altered to meet the needs of any denomination. Some basic elements that could be a part of any service are as follows:

First, it is a service of healing *and* thanksgiving, recognizing that we need to have time to praise God for the positive effects of the Holy Spirit.

Second, it is an ecumenical service where those outside of the church are welcome. This is important since there may not be a large number of churches in an area offering healing services.

Third, the service is based upon the Scriptures. James 5 was mentioned on more than one occasion during the service. The service follows the model of having the minister or elders lay hands upon the sick and pray.

Fourth, the gospel healings are read and discussed in ways that make them real to those present. Jesus' healings offer profound insights into our own situations. (The ability of the minister to bring these out was one of the high points of the service I described.)

Fifth, people are encouraged, but not required, to come forward to be healed. This is especially helpful for those who may be reluctant to come forward for prayer. The service provided a good balance between making people feel comfortable with coming forward but recognizing some may simply not want to and may want to seek healing where they are sitting.

Sixth, the issue of laying on of hands is handled appropriately. A person who has come forward is asked if it is okay to be touched, and is told where he or she will be touched.

Seventh, the healing prayer emphasizes the importance of creating changes in one's life. Healing is often not a one-time event. Many times people need to make very real and difficult changes in their lives.

Eighth, the healing prayer also acknowledges that there may be other forces involved in the affliction, and demands that these forces be driven out.

A final element I would mention is the presence of the Holy Spirit. I felt the Holy Spirit very profoundly in this service. This is more related to the devotion and genuineness of the people who helped with the service than anything else. God had come to this gathering.

This is a simple service, just as the method I outlined previously is simple. Both the service and the method are places in time where the healing power of God is acknowledged and sought. Something happens in surrendering yourself to God in daily life and in worship. That is the mysterious and wonderful power of the God who heals.

As we leave one another now, I pray that you seek the healing you need. I pray that you lay before God whatever brokenness you may feel. Open yourself to God's healing now, and know that there is ultimate peace and healing in the waiting arms of our Lord and Savior, Jesus Christ.

Exercise 8: Seek Healing

One of my favorite psalms reads, "Seek peace, and pursue it" (34:14). I like this psalm because it not only identifies a positive virtue, but it also encourages action. As you consider your healing now, I encourage you to take the same action. Seek healing. Look at what you want to be healed from, and use the methods mentioned to open yourself to healing. As you do this, look also for ways to become a healer yourself. Seeking healing and becoming a healer are positive ways of dealing with afflictions. They are ways we find the God who heals.

Notes

Notes to the Introduction

1. Rick Mathis, Ph.D., *The Christ-Centered Heart: Peaceful Living in Difficult Times* (Liguori, Mo.: Liguori/ Triumph, 1999).

Notes to Chapter One

1. These statistics are from the National Center for Health Statistic's Center for Disease Control and Prevention (1998). *FASTATS* [World Wide Web]. Available: <http://www.cdc.gov/nchswww/fastats/fastats.htm>.
2. Scott-Levin Associates, 1995, as quoted in A.F. Minor, Project Manager and Editor, *Source Book of Health Insurance Data, 1996* (Health Insurance Association of America, 1997), p. 119.

3. Health Insurance Association of America, 1995, as quoted in A.F. Minor, *Source Book of Health Insurance Data*, p. 159.

4. As quoted in Dale A. Matthews, M.D., with Connie Clark, *The Faith Factor: Proof of the Healing Power of Prayer* (New York: Viking, 1998), p. 83.

5. Matthew Kelty, *Sermons in a Monastery* (Kalamazoo, Mich.: Cistercian Publications, 1983), p. 59.

6. For another view of the message behind Saint Paul's failure to be healed from his thorn, see Francis MacNutt, Ph.D., *Healing* (Notre Dame, Ind.: Ave Maria Press, 1999), p. 66.

7. Kelty, *Sermons in a Monastery*, p. 39.

8. Ibid., pp. 46–47.

Notes to Chapter Two

1. For the healing acts of the disciples, including Saint Paul's own healing from blindness by Ananias, see Acts 3:1–16; 9:10; 9:32; 9:36; 14:8; 16:6; 20:7; 22:11; 28:3; 28:8.

Notes to Chapter Three

1. Dale A. Matthews, M.D., with Connie Clark, *The Faith Factor: Proof of the Healing Power of Prayer* (New York: Viking, 1998), p. 37.

2. Matthews, *The Faith Factor*, p. 25.

3. Ibid., p. 98.

4. Ibid., p. 135.

5. Larry Dossey, M.D., *Healing Words: The Power of Prayer and the Practice of Medicine* (San Francisco: HarperSanFrancisco, 1993), p. 2.

6. Larry Dossey, M.D., *Prayer Is Good Medicine* (San Francisco: HarperSanFrancisco, 1996), p. 4.

7. Dossey, *Healing Words*, p. 180.

8. Ibid., p. 180.

9. Ibid., pp. 190–95.

10. Ibid., p. 205.

11. Dean Ornish, M.D., *Love and Survival: The Scientific Basis for the Healing Power of Intimacy* (New York: HarperCollins Publishers, Inc., 1998), pp. 24–25.

12. Ornish, *Love and Survival*, p. 25.

13. Ibid., p. 25.

14. Ibid., pp. 2–3.

15. Ibid., p. 15 (emphasis added).

16. Ibid., p. 99.

17. Ibid., p. 3.

18. L. Gregory Jones, *Embodying Forgiveness: A Theological Analysis* (Grand Rapids, Mich.: William B. Eerdmans Publishing Company, 1995), p. 262.

19. Redford Williams, M.D., and Virginia Williams, Ph.D., *Anger Kills* (New York: Random House, 1993), p. 60.

20. Agnes Sanford, *The Healing Light* (New York: Ballantine Books, 1972), p. 45.

21. Sanford, *The Healing Light*, p. 46.

22. Francis MacNutt, Ph.D., *Healing* (Notre Dame, Ind.: Ave Maria Press, 1999), p. 124.

23. Jones, *Embodying Forgiveness,* p. 236. I am also indebted to Michael Battle of Duke Divinity School for a series of lectures he presented on the craft of forgiveness.

24. Jones, *Embodying Forgiveness* , p. 301.

Notes to Chapter Four

1. Robert Klitzman, M.D., *Being Positive: The Lives of Men and Women with HIV* (Chicago: Ivan R. Dee, 1997), p. 37.

2. Klitzman, *Being Positive*, p. 187.

3. Ibid., p. 189.

4. Ibid., p. 73.

5. Ibid., p. 124.

6. Ibid., p. 107.

7. See, for example, Gregory White Smith and Steven Naifeh, *Making Miracles Happen* (Boston: Little, Brown and Company, 1997). Smith and Naifeh cite numerous instances in which those playing an active role in their healthcare, even to the point of being bothersome to their physicians, have better outcomes.

8. Sidney J. Winawer, M.D., with Nick Taylor, *Healing Lessons* (Boston: Little, Brown and Company, 1998), p. 150.

9. Winawer, *Healing Lessons*, p. 258.

10. Ibid., p. 168.

11. David Brazier, *The Feeling Buddha* (New York: From International, 1998), pp. 36, 101, and 185–87.

12. See, for example, Martin E.P. Seligman, *Learned Optimism* (New York: Albert A. Knopf, 1991).

13. See, for example, Richard Carlson, *You Can Be Happy No Matter What* (Novato, Calif.: New World Library, 1997).

Notes to Chapter Five

1. Richard P. Brennan, *Dictionary of Scientific Literacy* (New York: John Wiley & Sons, Inc., 1992), p. 138.

2. Brennan, *Dictionary of Scientific Literacy*, p. 139.

3. Fred Alan Wolff, *Taking the Quantum Leap: The New Physics for Non-Scientists* (New York: Harper & Row, 1989), p. 225.

4. Agnes Sanford, *Sealed Orders* (Plainfield, N.J.: Logos International, 1972), p. 12.

5. Agnes Sanford, *The Healing Light* (New York: Ballantine Books, 1972), p. 2.

6. Agnes Sanford, *The Healing Gifts of the Spirit* (San Francisco: HarperSanFrancisco, 1984), p. 62.

7. Sanford, *The Healing Gifts of the Spirit*, p. 63.

8. Ibid., pp. 56–57.

9. Sanford, *The Healing Light*, p. 26.

10. Ibid., p. 163.

11. Ibid., p. 14.

12. Ibid., p. 60.

13. Ibid., p. 46.

14. Ibid., p. 56.

15. Ibid., p. 57.

16. Sanford, *The Healing Gifts of the Spirit*, p. 97.

17. Bridget Meehan, *The Healing Power of Prayer* (Liguori, Mo.: Liguori Publications, 1995).

18. Meehan, *The Healing Power of Prayer*, pp. 44–45.

19. Kamila Blessing, *It Was a Miracle* (Minneapolis: Augsburg Fortress, 1999), p. 119.

20. Blessing, *It Was a Miracle*, p. 120.

21. Ibid., p. 120.

Notes to Chapter Six

1. Dean Ornish, M.D., *Love and Survival: 8 Pathways to Intimacy and Health* (New York: HarperPerennial, 1998), p. 71.

2. Ornish, *Love and Survival*, p. 130.

3. Ibid., p. 131.

4. Ibid., p. 130.

5. Allan Luks with Peggy Payne, *The Healing Power of Doing Good: The Health and Spiritual Benefits of Helping Others* (New York: Fawcett Columbine, 1991), pp. 17–18.

6. Luks and Payne, *The Healing Power of Doing Good*, p. 82.

7. Ibid., pp. 151–56.

8. I came across this statement in Richard Nelson Bolles' *The 1995 What Color Is Your Parachute* (Berkeley, Calif.: Ten Speed Press, 1995), p. 460. This is in a section of the book entitled, "How to Find Your Mission in Life," which contains a great many insights consistent with becoming a *healing* healer.

Notes to Chapter Seven

1. Agnes Sanford, *The Healing Light* (New York: Ballantine Books, 1972), p. 6.

2. Francis MacNutt, Ph.D., *Healing* (Notre Dame, Ind.: Ave Maria Press, 1999), p. 161.

3. MacNutt, Ph.D., *Healing*, p. 162.

4. Ibid., pp. 193–204.

5. Brother David Steindl-Rast, *Gratefulness, the Heart of Prayer* (New York: Paulist Press, 1984), p. 224.

6. Esther de Waal, *Living With Contradiction: An Introduction to Benedictine Spirituality* (Harrisburg, Pa: Morehouse Publishing, 1997), p. 12.

7. Frank Bianco, *Voices of Silence: Lives of the Trappists Today* (New York, Paragon House, 1990).

8. Kathleen Norris, *The Cloister Walk* (New York: Riverhead Books, 1996).

9. de Waal, *Living With Contradiction*, p. 69.

10. Saint Benedict, *The Rule of Saint Benedict in English*, edited by Timothy Fry, O.S.B. (Collegeville, Minn.: The Liturgical Press, 1982), p. 18.

11. Harold G. Koenig, M.D., *The Healing Power of Faith* (New York: Simon & Schuster, 1999), pp. 88–89, 93.

Notes to Chapter Eight

1. Francis MacNutt, Ph.D., *Healing* (Notre Dame, Ind.: Ave Maria Press, 1999), p. 116.
2. MacNutt, Ph.D., *Healing*, p. 102.

About the Author

RICK MATHIS MANAGES medical policy research for Blue Cross Blue Shield of Tennessee. He received a Ph.D. in political science from Johns Hopkins University and has taught courses at Loyola College in Baltimore and at the University of Tennessee in Chattanooga. He lectures and writes on topics as varied as Thomas Merton, healthcare, and ethics and politics. A lifelong student of philosophy and Christian spirituality, he likes to focus on the application of spirituality to everyday life. He lives in Soddy-Daisy, Tennessee, with his wife, Karen. They have two children.

This book—*Prayer-Centered Healing: Finding the God Who Heals*—and its author are the recipients of the second Louis G. Miller Award, sponsored by Liguori Publications in honor of Louis G. Miller, long-time editor of *Liguorian* magazine (1961–1976) and pioneer of Catholic publishing.